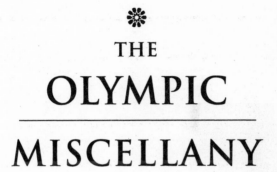

THE
OLYMPIC
MISCELLANY

Dedication

I wish to dedicate this book to two very good friends of mine –
both athletes in their own right! – Bill Clarkson and Mike Hartley
from Dukinfield, Manchester.

Thanks for all your support, boys.

Yours in sport

John

This edition published in 2008

Copyright © Carlton Books Limited 2008

Carlton Books Limited
20 Mortimer Street
London W1T 3JW

A CIP catalogue record for this book is available from the British Library

ISBN: 978-1-85375-659-7

Editor: Martin Corteel
Project Art Editor: Paul Chattaway
Production: Lisa Cook

Printed in Great Britain

THE
OLYMPIC

MISCELLANY

JOHN WHITE

WITH A FOREWORD BY DAME MARY PETERS

❋ FOREWORD ❋

I was delighted when John approached me to write the foreword to his book. As a youngster growing up in Liverpool I enjoyed an outdoor life. I had a brother, John, who was three years older than me, and everything he did I tried to do a little better. I was a bit of a tomboy and, looking back, I suppose the Olympic ideology was in me from an early age: *Citius, Altius, Fortius* ("Faster, Higher, Stronger"). In 1950, my father's business meant we had to move to Northern Ireland to live, and while a pupil at Ballymena Intermediate School I won my first trophy, a shield for the best all-round athlete. When we moved to Armagh a few years later my headmaster at Portadown College recognized that I had a certain degree of athletic potential and introduced me to the school's athletics coach, Kenneth McClelland. Ken coached me in the sprints, high jump and long jump and encouraged me to participate in the inaugural Northern Ireland pentathlon competition. I finished third behind Thelma Hopkins and Maeve Kyle, both Olympians.

I took part in my first Olympic Games in Tokyo in 1964, finishing fourth in the pentathlon. My athletics career blossomed after Tokyo and I managed a silver medal in the shot put at the 1966 Commonwealth Games and was very honoured to be named the Ladies GB Team Captain for the 1968 Olympics in Mexico City. I had a disappointing Games in Mexico, finishing ninth in the pentathlon. However, at the 1970 Commonwealth Games I managed a double gold, winning the pentathlon and the shot put. And so on to the 1972 Olympics in Munich ... Much has been written about my gold medal success in the pentathlon. My own memories from Munich are beating the home favourite, Heidi Rosendahl, albeit by just 10 points, and achieving four personal bests on my way to setting a new world record score of 4,801 points for the event. Two years later I retained my Commonwealth Games gold medal.

Although Munich was my final Olympiad as a competitor, my Olympic experiences were far from over. I worked for BBC Radio at the Montreal Olympics in 1976 and was the GB Ladies Team Manager for the Moscow Olympics in 1980 and the Los Angeles Olympics in 1984. In 1988 I covered the Seoul Olympics for New Zealand Radio, and I attended the following four Olympiads as a voluntary representative of the British Olympic Association. Sport has been my life and it has been good to me, while I have also had the privilege of meeting so many wonderful people. My success in Munich helped me raise the monies to build the Mary Peters Track and set up the Ulster Sports Trust, which assists up-and-coming young Northern Ireland athletes. And, who knows, we may even see one of these young men or women standing on a podium at the 2012 Olympics in London with a gold medal proudly hanging around their neck. That would be nice.

Dame Mary Peters, DBE

✳ ACKNOWLEDGEMENTS ✳

All Olympic gold medal winners have someone helping them, whether it is a coach, a physio, a training partner or indeed a team. My wife Janice and my sons Marc and Paul were my team.

I wish to express my thanks to my team for the help and support they gave me while I was writing this book.

Forever Yours
John

❊ INTRODUCTION ❊

We all have our own abiding memories of the "Greatest Show on Earth", while past Olympiads have provided the world with some truly remarkable achievements and unfortunately some distasteful incidents. My own memories from previous Games go back to 1972 and Mary Peters winning the gold medal in the pentathlon. We called her "Our Golden Girl" because, although she was born in Liverpool, Mary spent most of her life in Northern Ireland where I was born. And I was extremely proud and honoured when Dame Mary Peters, sorry Mary P, agreed to write the foreword to my book. Thanks, Our Mary!

So I hope that reading this book brings back many wonderful sporting memories for you, whether it is Jesse Owens and his sweep of four gold medals at the 1936 Olympics in Berlin, dubbed the "Hitler Olympics"; Ann Packer's gold medal in the 800 metres at the 1964 Olympic Games in Tokyo; David Hemery's gold medal success in the 400 metres hurdles at the 1968 Mexico City Olympics; Mark Spitz's haul of seven gold medals at Munich in 1972; Olga Korbut and Nadia Comaneci gliding effortlessly across our television screens at Montreal in 1976 with Nadia scoring the first ever perfect 10; the Coe–Ovett confrontations at Moscow in 1980; the magnificent performances of Carl Lewis at Los Angeles in 1984; the smiles of Linford Christie and Sally Gunnell after winning gold at Barcelona in 1992 or Kelly Holmes's double gold medal win at the 2004 Games in the city were the Olympics began in 776 BC, Athens. Whatever your own memory, enjoy.

John White

❋ THE GAMES OF THE I OLYMPIAD ❋

On 6 April 1896, His Majesty King George I officially opened the inaugural modern Olympic Games. Fittingly, Athens played host to the Games of the I Olympiad. A total of 241 athletes (all male) from 14 different countries participated in 43 events across nine sports. France, Great Britain, Germany and the host nation, Greece, had the highest number of delegates. Winners were presented with a silver medal and an olive branch. The closing ceremony took place on 15 April 1896.

Athens 1896 – Final Medals Table (Top 10)

Pos.	Nation	Gold	Silver	Bronze	Total
1	United States	11	7	2	20
2	Greece	10	17	19	46
3	Germany	6	5	2	13
4	France	5	4	2	11
5	Great Britain	2	3	2	7
6	Hungary	2	1	3	6
7	Austria	2	1	2	5
8	Australia	2	0	0	2
9	Denmark	1	2	3	6
10	Switzerland	1	2	0	3

❋ THE FLYING DANE ❋

At the 1960 Rome Olympics, Denmark's Paul Elvstrom won a fourth consecutive gold medal in sailing. In 1948 he won the Freefly class and then in 1952, 1956 and 1960 he claimed the gold medal in the Finn class. Elvstrom revolutionized dinghy sailing by pioneering the technique of "hiking" (also known as "sitting out"); he was the first to fix straps (toe-straps) in the bottom of his dinghy, and he also invented the "kicking strap". The kicking strap in particular helped the boat to go faster as it kept the sail flatter, allowing it to maximize the wind, leaving his competitors scratching their heads in puzzlement over how he managed to reach such high speeds. However, before he came ashore he removed all evidence of the straps, knowing only too well that his competitors would inspect his dinghy.

❋ OAK TREES FOR THE WINNERS ❋

In addition to a medal the athletes at the 1936 Berlin Olympics were presented with a winner's crown and an oak tree in a pot.

✻ A LATE ENTRY ✻

At the Atlanta Olympics tennis player Virag Csurgo was entered in the doubles event for Hungary. On the morning of 24 July 1996, she was warming up with a team-mate when one of the Hungarian team officials approached her and informed her that one of the singles entrants had failed to show up and Csurgo could replace her in the singles tournament if she could reach the court in time for the first-round match – beginning in five minutes. Csurgo ran to the venue, still wearing her practice T-shirt and shorts, and beat her Polish opponent, Aleksandra Olsza, 6–2, 7–5. However, she lost her second-round match 6–2, 6–3 to the number eight seed from Japan, Kimiko Date. The final was won by Lindsay Davenport of the USA, who defeated Arantxa Sanchez-Vicario from Spain 7–6, 6–2.

✻ GB DISAPPPOINTMENT ✻

Great Britain had a disappointing Games in 1996, winning just one gold medal thanks to the heroics of Matthew Pinsent and Steve Redgrave in the coxless pairs. Jonathan Edwards was the favourite to claim the triple jump gold medal but had to settle for silver following a series of uncharacteristic foul jumps. Linford Christie could not follow up his triumph in Barcelona four years earlier and was disqualified from the 100 metres final after being held culpable for two false starts. Christie argued with the officials, demanding to be reinstated, and when they refused he went on a "lap of honour" to noisy jeering from the crowd. Christie later claimed that they were booing the officials' decision and not him.

✻ HAND-IN-HAND ✻

At the 1992 Olympics in Barcelona, Derartu Tulu from Ethiopia won the 10,000 metres final to become the first female black African Olympic champion. In the final lap of the race Derartu Tulu took the lead and went on to win with Elana Meyer, a white South African, finishing second and Lynn Jennings (USA) third. When Meyer crossed the finish line Tulu took her opponent's hand and the two athletes set off on a victory lap, symbolizing a fresh start for a new Africa.

✻ LAND OF THE RISING SUN ✻

The 1912 Stockholm Olympics witnessed the first participation of Japan.

❈ OLYMPIC TALK (1) ❈

"When I came back to my native country, after all the stories about Hitler, I couldn't ride in the front of the bus. I had to go to the back door. I couldn't live where I wanted. I wasn't invited to shake hands with Hitler, but I wasn't invited to the White House to shake hands with the President, either."
Jesse Owens, winner of four gold medals at the 1936 Olympics, following reports that Hitler refused to shake his hand at the Games.

❈ OLYMPIA REVISITED ❈

At Athens in 2004 Kristin Heaston of the USA became the first woman to compete at the ancient site of Olympia when she took the first throw in the ladies' shot put event. However, it was Cuba's Yumileidi Cumba who became the first woman to win a gold medal at Olympia with a throw of 19.59 metres.

❈ SOVIET UNION'S BRIGHTEST STAR ❈

Gymnast Larysa Latynina of the Soviet Union remains the only athlete in any sport to have won 18 Olympic medals in her career. Her tally comprises nine gold, five silver and four bronze medals. In addition, she is one of only four athletes to have won nine Olympic gold medals and is the only athlete to have won 14 medals in individual events. Latynina is also one of only three women to have won the same Summer Olympics event three times (the floor exercise in 1956, 1960 and 1964). Her impressive medal haul reads: women's artistic gymnastics team gold (1956), all-around gold (1956), vault gold (1956), floor exercise gold (1956), uneven bars silver (1956), team portable apparatus bronze (1956), women's artistic gymnastics team gold (1960), all-around gold (1960), floor exercise gold (1960), uneven bars silver (1960), balance beam silver (1960), vault bronze (1960), women's artistic gymnastics team gold (1964), floor exercise gold (1964), all-around silver (1964), vault silver (1964), uneven bars bronze (1964) and balance beam bronze (1964). She also won 13 medals at World Championships.

❈ THE OLYMPIC RELAY ❈

The athletics events at the London Games of 1908 included for the first time a relay (entitled "the Olympic relay"). The athletes ran 200m, 200m, 400m and 800m.

❋ OLYMPIC CURSE FOR THE SEOUL MAN ❋

On 26 May 1984, Soviet pole vaulter Sergei Bubka broke the world record in Bratislava with a vault of 5.90 metres and then broke it twice more, raising it to 5.88 and 5.90 metres, the latter being achieved in London on 13 July 1984, just 15 days before the start of the Los Angeles Olympic Games. However, Bubka was unable to compete in LA when the USSR led a communist bloc boycott of the Games. Pierre Quinon from France won the pole vault gold medal at the Los Angeles Olympics with a vault 12cm lower than Bubka's world record. It was at Seoul in 1988 that Bubka won his only Olympic medal, taking the gold with a vault of 5.90 metres – but only just, as it was his third and final attempt. When the Olympics were held in Barcelona in 1992, Bubka entered the Games having just raised the world record to 6.11 metres in Dijon on 13 June. However, his Olympic curse struck when he failed to clear the bar in his first three attempts and went out of the competition. Four years later in Atlanta at the 1996 Olympics, a heel injury forced him to withdraw from the competition without making a single vault, and then at Sydney in 2000 he was disqualified from the final after three failed attempts to clear 5.70 metres. During his career Bubka won an impressive array of medals in the sport, claiming six consecutive IAAF World Championship gold medals (1983–97) and one European Championships gold medal (Stuttgart 1986). Segei Bubka broke the men's pole vault world record 35 times in his career, 17 times outdoor and 18 times indoor. "I love the pole vault because it is a professor's sport," Bubka once said. "One must not only run and jump, but one must think. Which pole to use, which height to jump, which strategy to use. I love it because the results are immediate and the strongest is the winner. Everyone knows it. In everyday life that is difficult to prove."

❋ MARK'S CHARISMA ❋

At the 1988 Games Mark Todd, riding Charisma, retained his three-day individual Olympic title to become the first rider to win successive individual three-day-event titles for 60 years. He also won one silver and two bronze medals during his career as well as recording three wins in the prestigious Badminton Horse Trials and five in the Burghley Three-Day Trials. Mark also won team gold medals with New Zealand at the 1990 and 1998 World Championships and at the 1997 European Championships (when the competition was open to the world).

Lane No./Athlete	Country	Olympic Medals
1 Carl Lewis	USA	2 Gold – Los Angeles 1984 & Seoul 1988
2 Archie Hahn	USA	2 Gold – St Louis 1904 & Athens 1906*
3 Jesse Owens	USA	Gold – Berlin 1936
4 Linford Christie	GB	Gold – Barcelona 1992, Silver – Seoul 1988
5 Maurice Greene	USA	Gold – Sydney 2000, Silver – Athens 2004
6 Valeri Borzov	USSR	Gold – Moscow 1980, Bronze – Montreal 1976
7 Charlie Paddock	USA	Gold – Antwerp 1920
8 Harold Abrahams	GB	Gold – Paris 1924

* Intercalated Games

✳ A POPULAR WINNER ✳

Spyridon Louis, a Greek shepherd, pleased the host nation of the Games when he raced to victory in the marathon. Louis was born on 12 January 1873 in Maroussi, near Athens. Of all the events at the first modern Olympiad the hosts wanted to win the 40,000m marathon race more than any other. The endurance race was specifically created in honour of the legend of Pheidippides, a Greek hero who allegedly carried the news of the Greek victory at the Battle of Marathon in 490 BC by running from Marathon to Athens. With four kilometres left to race, Louis took the lead in a field of 17 runners and to the delight of the 100,000 spectators located in and around the Panathenaic Stadium he won the marathon by more than seven minutes. Some 40 years after his famous victory Louis recalled the moments directly after he crossed the winning line: "That hour was something unimaginable and it still appears to me in my memory like a dream … Twigs and flowers were raining down on me. Everybody was calling out my name and throwing their hats in the air." Louis remained a national hero until his death on 26 March 1940. He participated in only one Olympic Games. Louis did not own any shoes, and to race in the Olympic marathon he wore shoes paid for by people from local villages.

✳ GREATEST EVER WRESTLER ✳

In 1964 24-year-old Japanese wrestler Osamu Watanabe delighted his home nation by winning the gold medal in the freestyle featherweight division. It was his first Olympiad. Amazingly, Watanabe went through the competition without giving up any points (his aggregate score was 186–0) and spent only 10 minutes on the mats on his way to claiming gold. After the Games he retired, making him the only modern Olympian in any style of wrestling to go unbeaten throughout the entirety of his career and without conceding any points.

✳ SUPER EAGLES SWOOP TO TAKE GOLD ✳

Each team that qualified for the football tournament at Atlanta was permitted to include three professional players, regardless of age or previous Olympic experience. The men's tournament was won by Nigeria (nicknamed the "Super Eagles"), with Argentina claiming the silver medal and Brazil the bronze. In the women's tournament the USA won the gold.

❊ THE GAMES OF THE II OLYMPIAD ❊

On 14 May 1900, the Games of the II Olympiad officially opened in Paris, France. The Games were held as part of the Exposition Universelle Internationale, also known as the Paris World's Fair. Four years after the staging of the inaugural modern Olympics women made their first appearance in the Games. A total of 997 athletes (975 male, 22 female) from 24 different countries participated in 95 events across 18 sports. The organizers of the Exposition/World's Fair spread the 95 Olympic events over a period of five months, and the closing ceremony took place on 28 October. As a result the Olympic status of the events was so low profile that many athletes died without ever knowing that they had actually participated in an Olympics.

Paris 1900 – Final Medals Table (Top 10)

Pos.	Nation	Gold	Silver	Bronze	Total
1	France	26	41	34	101
2	United States	19	14	14	47
3	Great Britain	15	6	9	30
4	Mixed Team	6	3	3	12
5	Switzerland	6	2	1	9
6	Belgium	5	2	2	9
7	Germany	4	2	2	8
8	Italy	2	1	0	3
9	Australia	2	0	3	5
10	Denmark	1	3	2	6
	Hungary	1	3	2	6

❊ A WHOLE NEW BALL GAME ❊

The programme for the Berlin Games of 1936 included men's handball and basketball tournaments. In the basketball final, the USA beat neighbours Canada 19–8 with the game played outdoors on a dirt pitch in heavy rain. As a result of the sodden surface the players were unable to dribble with the ball, hence the low score, while the 1,000 spectators were forced to stand as the organizers did not provide any seating.

❊ GREEK JUDOKAN CHAMPION ❊

Ilias Iliadis won Greece's first ever gold medal in judo when he claimed the men's 81kg category at the Athens Olympics in 2004.

✻ THE THORPEDO ✻

At the Sydney Games the home favourite, Ian Thorpe, won the gold medal in the 400 metres freestyle, breaking his own world record. The 17-year-old Australian swimmer, nicknamed "Thorpedo", then swam the anchor leg in the 4x100m freestyle relay and helped his country to gold. Thorpe claimed his third gold at the Olympiad in the 4x200m freestyle relay and added a silver medal in the 200m freestyle.

✻ THE MUNICH MASSACRE ✻

At 4.30 a.m. on 5 September 1972, with just six days of competition remaining in the Games of the XX Olympiad, eight members of the Palestinian terrorist organization known as Black September (with links to Yasser Arafat's Fatah organization) slipped into the Olympic Village under cover of night and killed two Israeli team members. They then held nine other members of the Israeli team hostage in their team apartment quarters. The subsequent siege lasted almost 18 hours and ended at Furstenfeldbruck military airport when a failed rescue attempt resulted in the deaths of the nine remaining athletes, a German policeman and five of the terrorists. The three surviving terrorists were captured but later released by West Germany following the hijacking of a Lufthansa airliner. The Games were suspended temporarily but continued after a day of mourning. The Munich Massacre resulted in West Germany readdressing its approach to combating terrorism and the creation of "GSG-9", an elite counter-terrorist unit. Meanwhile, the Israeli government was swift to exact revenge and launched two aggressive counter-terrorism programmes known as "Operation Wrath of God" and "Operation Spring of Youth". The Israelis launched air strikes on Palestine and systematically hunted down and assassinated the remaining terrorists and those who plotted the Munich Massacre.

✻ FINN PLAYS SECOND FIDDLE TO FINN ✻

Ville Ritola (Finland) won the 10,000 metres at the 1924 Games, breaking his own world record by 12 seconds in the process. He also won the 3,000 metres steeplechase – by 75 metres – the cross-country team event and the 3,000 metres team event. He also claimed two silver medals, finishing behind his fellow countryman, Paavo Nurmi, in the 5,000 metres and in the cross-country race. He was outshone overall by Nurmi, who won five gold medals at the Games.

❋ JESSE OWENS (1913–80) ❋

James Cleveland ("Jesse") Owens was born on 12 September 1913 in Oakville, Alabama, USA. The youngest of ten children, he was just eight years old when his family moved to Cleveland, Ohio. One day at Fairview Junior High School the athletics coach, Charlie Riley, timed the pupils in the 60-yard dash and was so amazed by Jesse's time that he asked him to join the school's track team. When Jesse explained that he could not train with the team after school because he had a job, Riley agreed to train Jesse early in the morning. As a senior at Cleveland East Technical High School Jesse tied the world record in the 100 metres with a time of 9.4 seconds. In 1933 Jesse tied the 100m world record again while running in the National High School Championships in Chicago and also leapt a distance of 24 feet, 9½ inches (7.56m) in the long jump. Many colleges and universities attempted to lure Jesse to join their athletics team, but he chose Ohio State University after they agreed to help his father find employment.

Affectionately known as the "Buckeye Bullet", Jesse won a record eight individual NCAA Championships, four in 1935 and another four in 1936. Indeed, Jesse's record of four gold medals at a single NCAA Championships has only ever been equalled by Xavier Carter (in 2006). During his time at Ohio State University Jesse was forced to live off campus with other African-American athletes, and when he travelled with the team he was forced to order take-away food or eat at "blacks only" restaurants and to sleep in "blacks only" hotels.

At the 1936 Berlin Olympics, Jesse won four gold medals: in the 100 metres, the 200 metres, the long jump and the 4x400m relay. In all but one of these events Jesse broke the Olympic record. When he returned to the USA he received a ticker-tape welcome in New York, but because of the discrimination against "Negroes" in the USA at the time, when Jesse went to the Waldorf-Astoria hotel to attend a dinner being held in his honour he was forced to take a freight elevator. Just as disgracefully, because he was black he was not offered any endorsement deals in the USA. Therefore, in order to support his family Jesse became a "runner for hire", racing against people, horses, even motorcycles. In 1976 Jesse was awarded the highest honour a civilian can receive in the USA when President Gerald Ford awarded him the Presidential Medal of Freedom.

Did You Know That?
The Jesse Owens Memorial Stadium, a multi-sport facility, was opened in 2001 on the Ohio State University campus.

❋ OLYMPIC TALK (2) ❋

"I declare the opening of the first international Olympic Games in Athens. Long live the Nation. Long live the Greek people."
King George I of Greece, at the inaugural Modern Games of 1896

❋ PEACE TO ALL ❋

Antwerp 1920 was the first Games in which doves were released to symbolize peace. The Games came just two years after the end of the First World War, in which 28 countries had been involved and almost 10 million soldiers had lost their lives in four years. In the scheduled four-year cycle of Olympiads, Berlin 1916 would have been the Games of the VI Olympiad and is still counted in the sequence even though they were not held.

❋ THE UPSET OF ALL UPSETS ❋

At Atlanta 1996 the US men's 4x100m team failed to win the gold medal for the first time in their history at an Olympiad in which they competed in the event. Team Canada took the gold medal, with the USA claiming the silver and Brazil the bronze.

❋ THE FLYING KIWI ❋

At the Tokyo Games New Zealand's Peter Snell retained his Olympic title in the 800 metres and also claimed gold in the 1500 metres. Despite a relatively short career, which also saw him set five world records (800 metres, 800 yards, 1,000 metres, 1500 metres and the mile) he was voted New Zealand's "Sports Champion of the 20th Century". It would be 41 years before Snell's 800m/1500m gold medal double was equalled in open global championship, when Rashid Ramzi of Bahrain won both middle-distance events at the 2005 Athletics World Championships held in Helsinki, Finland.

❋ THE MIGHTY MAGYARS ❋

At the 1952 Olympics Hungary's "Golden Team" (nicknamed the "Magical Magyars") won the gold medal in the football tournament, defeating Yugoslavia 2–0 in the final. This was the team which played a record-breaking 33 international games without defeat between 14 May 1950 and 4 July 1954 – a record which still stands. Hungary also won the football gold medal at the 1964 and 1968 Olympics.

※ YOUNGEST EVER GOLD MEDALLIST ※

At the Los Angeles Games of 1932, 14-year-old Kusuo Kitamura of Japan won the 1500m freestyle swimming gold medal (in a time of 19:12.40) to become the youngest male in any sport ever to win an Olympic gold medal in an individual event.

※ BACK FROM THE DEAD ※

The Amsterdam Games of 1928 broke new ground for female athletes. The 100 metres was the first women's track event to be contested in Olympic history and was won by Betty Robinson (USA) in a time equalling the world record. She also won a silver medal in the 4x100m relay. Amazingly, Robinson had competed in her first 100m race only four months before the 1928 Olympics, and this was only the fourth track meet of her athletics career. In her first outdoor track meeting the 16-year-old American schoolgirl finished second to the USA record holder, and in her next race she equalled the world record for 100 metres, but her time was not officially recognized. In 1931 Robinson was so severely injured in a plane crash that the man who found her among the wreckage thought she was dead. He placed her body in the boot of his car and drove to the local mortuary – where the mortician discovered that she was still alive. Robinson remained unconscious for seven weeks, and her injuries were so severe she could not walk normally for almost two years. Remarkably, Robinson still wanted to return to competitive sprinting, but the injuries she sustained in the crash restricted the movement of her leg as she was unable to bend her leg fully at the knee. This meant that she could not take up the crouched starting position for the 100 metres. Undaunted by this, she concentrated on running in relays, and in 1936 she "came back from the dead" and won a second gold medal as a member of the USA's 4x100m relay team at the Berlin Olympics.

※ FIRST BLACK GOLD IN THE POOL ※

During the 1988 Seoul Olympics, Surinam's Anthony Nesty won his country's first-ever Olympic medal when he claimed gold in the 100 metres butterfly. He was not only the first black swimmer in history to win an Olympic gold medal but also only the second black swimmer to win an Olympic medal following Enith Sijtje Maria Brigitha (Netherlands), who won two bronze medals (100m freestyle and 200m freestyle) at Montreal in 1976.

❊ THE OLYMPIC OATH ❊

The Olympic oath was composed by Baron Pierre de Coubertin, the founder of the modern Olympic Games. It was first taken by an athlete at the 1920 Summer Olympics in Antwerp. The first officials' oath was taken at the 1972 Summer Olympics in Munich. Over the past 87 years the actual wording of the oath has altered slightly. The oath read by Victor Boin in 1920 was: "We swear we will take part in the Olympic Games in a spirit of chivalry, for the honour of our country and for the glory of sport." In subsequent years the word "swear" was replaced by "promise" and "country" was replaced by "team". In 2000 reference to doping was included in the oath.

Speakers
The athletes and judges who have delivered the Olympic oath at the Summer Olympic Games are as follows:

Olympics	Olympic Oath Athlete	Judge
1920 Antwerp	Victor Boin	-
1924 Paris	Georges André	-
1928 Amsterdam	Harry Dénis	-
1932 Los Angeles	George Calnan	-
1936 Berlin	Rudolf Ismayr	-
1948 London	Don Finlay	-
1952 Helsinki	Heikki Savolainen	-
1956 Melbourne	John Landy	
	Henri Saint Cyr	-
1960 Rome	Adolfo Consolini	-
1964 Tokyo	Takashi Ono	-
1968 Mexico City	Pablo Garrido	-
1972 Munich	Heidi Schüller	Heinz Pollay
1976 Montreal	Pierre St-Jean	Maurice Fauget
1980 Moscow	Nikolay Andrianov	Aleksandr Medved
1984 Los Angeles	Edwin Moses	Sharon Weber
1988 Seoul	Hur Jae	Lee Hak-Rae
1992 Barcelona	Luis Doreste Blanco	Eugeni Asensio
1996 Atlanta	Teresa Edwards	Hobie Billingsly
2000 Sydney	Rechelle Hawkes	Peter Kerr
2004 Athens	Zoe Dimoschaki	Lazaros Voreadis

❊ MONEY-MAKING VENTURE ❊

Total ticket revenues for the 1936 Games in Berlin amounted to 7.5 million marks, with a nominal profit in excess of 1 million marks.

THE GAMES OF THE III OLYMPIAD

On 1 July 1904, the Games of the III Olympiad were officially opened in St Louis, Missouri, by David Francis, President of the Louisiana Purchase Exposition at Francis Field (also known as the World's Fair). A total of 651 athletes (645 male, 6 female) from 12 different countries participated in 91 events across 17 sports. The closing ceremony was held on 23 November 1904. Originally Chicago, Illinois, had bid successfully to host the 1904 Summer Olympics, but the organizers of the Exposition refused to permit a rival event to take place at the same time. The organizing committee behind the Exposition began to draw up a schedule of its own sporting events and wrote to the organizing committee of the Chicago bid informing them that unless the Games were moved to St Louis the Exposition intended to overshadow the 1904 Olympic Games. President Theodore Roosevelt backed the St Louis bid, as the World's Fair was going to showcase the world's newest technologies, from automobiles to electricity. Eventually Baron Pierre de Coubertin buckled under the pressure and Chicago lost out.

St Louis 1904 – Final Medals Table (Top 10)

Pos.	*Nation*	*Gold*	*Silver*	*Bronze*	*Total*
1	United States	78	82	79	239
2	Germany	4	4	5	13
3	Cuba	4	2	3	9
4	Canada	4	1	1	6
5	Hungary	2	1	1	4
6	Great Britain	1	1	0	2
	Mixed Team	1	1	0	2
8	Greece	1	0	1	2
	Switzerland	1	0	1	2
10	Austria	0	0	1	1

STUDENT GOLD

Wyomia Tyus, a 19-year-old student from Tennessee State University, won the gold medal for the 100 metres at the 1964 Tokyo Olympic Games, having equalled Wilma Rudolph's (USA) world record during her heats. She also claimed a silver medal in the 4x100m relay. Four years later in Mexico City she won the 100m gold again to become the first woman to successfully defend the Olympic 100m title. Tyus set a new world record in the 1968 final and also won a gold medal in the 4x100m relay.

❈ LINFORD'S BAN ❈

Linford Christie (GB) tested positive for the banned stimulant Pseudoephredine at the Seoul Olympics, where he won two silver medals (100m and 4x100m relay), but was cleared by the IOC of any wrongdoing when it was discovered that the substance could have come from ginseng, a permitted herbal remedy. However, in 1999 during an indoor track meet in Germany Linford was found guilty of using the banned performance-enhancing drug Nandrolone following a routine doping test. Christie claimed that the illegal metabolites of the banned substance probably entered his system accidentally via the legal nutritional supplements he used in his diet. The sport's governing body, the IAAF, rejected his explanation and handed him a two-year ban despite UK Athletics giving Christie their support. Following the ban the British Olympic Association (BOA) stated that Linford would not be afforded accreditation at any future Olympic Games, although their "ban" did not prevent him from coaching or mentoring athletes. Christie was 39 years old at the time of the incident in Germany and always maintained his innocence: "If I took drugs there had to be a reason to take drugs. I had pretty much retired from the sport."

❈ JAPANESE RUNNER GOES MISSING ❈

During the 1912 Olympic marathon Japanese runner Shizo Kanakuri dropped out of the race near the town of Tureberg. He found a garden where he rested and was given refreshments by the owners of the house. The Swedish race officials were never informed that Kanakuri had withdrawn from the race, and it was not until 55 years later that Kanakuri was able to finish the marathon and run into the Olympic Stadium, which he did during a visit to Stockholm in 1967.

❈ EAST GERMANY'S WATER BABIES ❈

At the 1976 Olympics the East German women's swimming team were so dominant that they won 11 of the 13 gold medals on offer. The only two events in the pool they lost were the 200 metres backstroke, which was a 1–2–3 for the USSR, and the 4x100m relay, which was won by the USA (East Germany took the silver). In total the East German ladies won 11 golds, six silvers and one bronze. The East German men's swimming team, meanwhile, managed only one medal from their 13 events, a bronze for Roland Matthes in the 100 metres backstroke.

❈ OLYMPIC TALK (3) ❈

"I heard people yelling my name, and I couldn't realize how one fellow could have so many friends."
Jim Thorpe, double gold medal winner in 1912, speaking about receiving a ticker-tape welcome on Broadway

❈ OLYMPICS FIRST QUAD ❈

In 1900 US athlete Alvin Christian Kraenzlein became the first sportsman to win four Olympic titles in a single Games, and up to and including the 2004 Olympics he remains the only track and field athlete to achieve such a haul in individual events. Over the course of three days, Kraenzlein took the gold in the 60m, the 110m hurdles, the 200m hurdles and the long jump. In the 60 metres he ran both the preliminary round and the final round in 7.0 seconds. His long jump victory, in which he defeated the silver medallist, Myer Prinstein, by a single centimetre, was marred by controversy. Prinstein, the world record holder, had set his mark in the qualification round and, like his fellow American athletes, including Kraenzlein, he refused to compete in the final round because it was being held on a Sunday. However, Kraenzlein changed his mind, and when Prinstein learned that Kraenzlein had not only competed, but had also beaten his mark, he became violent and reportedly punched Kraenzlein. In 1901 Kraenzlein, the holder of six world records, hung up his track shoes and concentrated on a career as an athletics coach.

❈ LOSER FASTER THAN WINNER ❈

Los Angeles 1984 saw the introduction of two finals in the men's 400 metres freestyle. The eight fastest qualifiers took part in the "A" final and the next eight fastest swam in a consolation "B" final. However, much to the embarrassment of the IOC the winner of the "B" final, Thomas Fahrner (West Germany), recorded a faster time than the winner of the "A" final (George Dicarlo of the USA). The two-final set-up was discontinued after the 1996 Olympics in Atlanta.

❈ ALL OVER BEFORE IT STARTED ❈

The outdoor tennis tournament for the 1912 Stockholm Olympics started on 26 June and was completed the day before the opening ceremony.

❋ SPECIALLY BUILT "OLYMPIC" STADIA ❋

The following stadia were specifically built to play host to the Olympic Games and include the words "Olympic Stadium" in their name:

❖ Stockholms Olympiastadion – Stockholm (1912) ❖
❖ Olympisch Stadion – Antwerp (1920) ❖
❖ Stade Olympique de Colombes – Paris (1924) ❖
❖ Olympisch Stadion – Amsterdam (1928) ❖
❖ Olympiastadion – Berlin (1936) ❖
❖ Olympiastadion – Helsinki (1952) ❖
❖ Stadio Olimpico – (1964) ❖
❖ Olympiastadion – Munich (1972) ❖
❖ Le Stade Olympique – Montreal (1976) ❖
❖ Centennial Olympic Stadium – Atlanta (1996) ❖
❖ Olympiako Stadio Athinas "Spyros Louis" – Athens (2004) ❖
❖ Olympic Stadium – London (2012) ❖

❋ BASEBALL MEDALS AT LAST ❋

In 1992 baseball, which had previously appeared as a demonstration sport at six Olympiads, received full accreditation as a medals sport. Cuba won the gold medal, the silver went to Chinese Taipei, and the bronze was won by Japan. The USA finished fourth.

❋ LASSE THE GREAT ❋

In lap 12 of the 10,000 metres final at the 1972 Games, Lasse Viren of Finland fell and then got back on his feet to break Ron Clarke's seven-year-old world record for the distance and claim the gold medal. Viren's winning time was 27:38:40. Viren also won gold in the 5,000 metres to become only the fourth athlete in Olympic history to win both events at the same Olympiad, joining Hannes Kolehmainen (1912), Emil Zatopek (1952) and Vladimir Kuts (1956). Four years later, in Montreal, Viren won both events again, becoming the only repeat winner of the 5,000 metres in Olympic history. Amazingly, just 18 hours after the 5,000 metres final in Munich, he competed in the marathon and finished in fifth place in a highly respectable time of 2:13:11. Viren's Olympic career ended in Moscow in 1980 when he could manage only fifth place in the 10,000 metres and was outclassed by Miruts Yifter and the rest of the pack in the 5,000 metres over the final 300 metres of the race. Viren broke the world record at both two miles and 5,000m.

❋ THE PARADE OF THE DELEGATIONS ❋

During the opening ceremony of the 1908 London Olympics at the newly built White City Stadium in London, the athletes marched into the stadium by nation, as most countries sent selected national teams. This was the first time athletes had been paraded in sports uniforms walking behind the flag of their nation at the start of an Olympic Games, a tradition that was followed in subsequent Games and became known as the Parade of the Delegations (or Nations). However, in 1908 the infamous "Battle of Shepherd's Bush" occurred when the delegation from the USA noticed that there was no American flag among the national flags decorating the stadium for the opening ceremonies. Martin Sheridan, winner of the discus gold medal at the 1904 Olympics in St Louis and the 1908 flag bearer for the USA, responded by refusing to dip the Stars and Stripes when he passed King Edward VII's box during the Parade of the Delegations at the opening ceremony. "This flag dips to no earthly King," said Sheridan, who who was born in Treenduff, County Mayo, Ireland, and took gold in the discus and Greek discus at the 1908 Games. However, the US athletes were not the only ones to have a complaint over flags. At the time the Grand Duchy of Finland was ruled by Russia. When the Finnish athletes were informed that they would have to march into the stadium behind Russia's "Hammer and Sickle" flag they refused and elected to march with no flag at all. Similarly, Irish athletes were compelled to compete for the British team, and many of them withdrew from the ceremony rather than march behind the Union Jack. Meanwhile the Swedish flag had not been displayed above the stadium, and consequently the members of the Swedish team also decided not to take part in the opening ceremony. Although the custom is to dip the nation's flag as a sign of respect to heads of state attending the cermony, since 1908 US flag bearers have followed Sheridan's example by not doing so.

❋ 1956 GAMES BOYCOTT ❋

Two major international incidents resulted in six NOCs boycotting the 1956 Melbourne Games. As a direct result of the Suez Crisis, Egypt, Iraq and Lebanon declined their invitation to compete in the Games, and the Soviet Union's invasion of Hungary led to the withdrawal of the Netherlands, Spain and Switzerland. In addition, less than two weeks before the opening ceremony the People's Republic of China also withdrew from the Games because the Republic of China (under the name Formosa) had been permitted to compete.

❋ THE BEN JOHNSON SCANDAL ❋

At the 1987 IAAF World Championships held in Rome, Italy, Ben Johnson of Canada burst on to the athletics scene by beating Carl Lewis (USA) in the men's 100 metres final in a new world record time of 9.83 seconds. Lewis was devastated and knew he had a fight on his hands to retain his 100m Olympic title when Seoul hosted the Olympics in 1988. Johnson's preparations for the 1988 Olympics did not go to plan, as he suffered a few niggling injuries in the early part of 1988. Then, on 17 August 1988, Johnson faced his nemesis, Lewis, in Zurich, Switzerland, in their first meeting since the Rome championships. Lewis won the 100 metres in 9.93 seconds, while a disappointed Johnson could only finish third. After his victory Lewis taunted Johnson saying: "The gold medal for the [Olympic] 100 metres is mine. I will never again lose to Johnson." Thirty-eight days later came the race everyone wanted to see, the men's 100 metres Olympic final and a speed shootout between the American and the Canadian. Lewis was favourite to retain his 100m title, with the main challenger thought to be Great Britain's Linford Christie. Johnson just about made it into the final after looking "slow" in the heats and only coming through his quarter-final heat as the fastest loser. However, in the final Johnson just tore out of the blocks and ran like a rocket up the track, winning the gold medal and lowering his own world record time by 0.04 seconds to 9.79 seconds. As he crossed the finish line Johnson glanced to his left and raised his right arm in the air to celebrate victory. Lewis finished second and Christie was third. Canadians everywhere celebrated Johnson's success, and the papers carried headlines such as "Bentastic". After his victory Johnson told the media, "They can break my record, but they can't take my gold medal away", before adding that he could have run faster than 9.79 seconds had he not looked behind him and thrust his arm in the air. How wrong he was. As with all Olympic champions, Johnson was required to provide a urine sample after the race, and when the test results came back three days later the sample contained traces of the banned steroid Stanozolol, and Johnson was immediately stripped of his medal. Johnson went from hero to zero in just 72 hours and was now a disgraced athlete who had been caught cheating. The IOC awarded the gold medal to Carl Lewis, the silver medal to Linford Christie and moved Calvin Smith (USA) from fourth place to the bronze medal position. Johnson was handed a two-year ban from the sport, and when he later admitted to having used steroids when he ran his 1987 world record, the IAAF annulled his 9.83 seconds time as well as his 9.79 time.

❋ THE GAMES OF THE IV OLYMPIAD ❋

The 1908 London Olympics were officially opened on 27 April 1908 by HRH King Edward VII. The 1908 Olympics had originally been awarded to Rome, but were reassigned to London following an eruption of Mount Vesuvius, near Naples, on 7 April 1906. The Italian government needed money for urgent rebuilding in the disaster zone and applied to the IOC for the Games to be given to another city. The other two candidate cities who lost out to Rome to host the 1908 Games, Berlin and Milan, did not think they could organize the Olympics at only 18 months' notice. However, despite the lack of time, London's offer to host the Games was accepted by the IOC in November 1906. As it turned out, although the Games were held in conjunction with the Franco-British Exhibition, which at the time was a better known event than the Olympics, the 1908 Olympics were the best organized Games to date. The organization was helped greatly by the fact that many of the governing bodies of sports in Britain had already been in existence for many years. A total of 22 nations sent 2,008 athletes (1,971 men, 37 women) to participate in 110 events across 22 sports. The closing ceremony took place on 31 October 1908.

London 1908 – Final Medals Table (Top 10)

Pos.	Nation	Gold	Silver	Bronze	Total
1	Great Britain	56	51	38	145
2	United States	23	12	12	47
3	Sweden	8	6	11	25
4	France	5	5	9	19
5	Germany	3	5	6	14
6	Hungary	3	4	2	9
7	Canada	3	3	10	16
8	Norway	2	3	3	8
9	Italy	2	2	0	4
10	Belgium	1	5	2	8

❋ RECORD MEDAL HAUL ❋

Aliexander Dityatin (USSR) won a staggering eight medals in the eight gymnastics events he participated in at the 1980 Moscow Olympics. His medal haul was a record for a single Olympiad. Four years earlier in Montreal he won two silver medals, for the rings and the team event. Dityatin's record medal haul for a single Olympiad was equalled by swimmer Michael Phelps in Athens 2004.

❈ FOUR-WEEK GAMES INTRODUCED ❈

The Los Angeles Olympics were the shortest to date, lasting 16 days. Between 1900 and 1928, no Summer Olympics lasted less than 79 days, and since 1932 no Olympiad has lasted more than 18 days. The inaugural modern Games, at Athens in 1896, lasted only nine days.

❈ AMERICA'S SWIMMING QUEEN ❈

While Ireland's golden girl, Michelle Smith, claimed three gold medals in Atlanta, Amy Van Dyken from the USA went one better, winning four (50m freestyle, 100m butterfly, 4x100m freestyle relay & 4x100m medley relay). Her haul made her the first American female to win four gold medals in a single Olympiad.

❈ GDR CLEANS UP IN THE WATER ❈

At Moscow in 1980 the East German ladies dominated the pool, winning 11 of the 13 gold medals on offer. Only Michelle Ford of Australia in the 800 metres freestyle and the USSR's Lina Kaciusyte in the 200 metres prevented a clean sweep of gold medals for the GDR. They were so good that they completed a 1-2-3 in six of the events to claim 26 of the 35 medals available (excluding the silver and bronze medals in the two team events, where they won gold). On the East German men's swimming team only Jorg Woithe won a gold medal, in the 100 metres freestyle. In the rowing events the GDR were equally dominant, winning 11 of the 14 Olympic golds. Their men won seven out of eight events and were only denied a clean sweep by Finland's Pertti Karppinen, who successfully defended his single sculls title, while the women won four of their six events.

❈ DRAMATIC MARATHON FINISH ❈

The 1948 Olympic marathon witnessed a dramatic finish as Etienne Gailly of Belgium entered Wembley Stadium in first place with just a single lap (400 metres) of the gruelling race left to run. However, Gailly was so exhausted he could barely stay on his feet. He was overtaken by Delfo Cabrera of Argentina, who claimed the gold medal, and by Thomas Richards of Great Britain, who took the silver. Eventually Gailly managed to cross the line to win the bronze medal in a marathon finish all too reminiscent of Dorando Pietri's tragic near miss 40 years earlier.

❋ OLYMPIC TALK (4) ❋

"Scientists have proven that it's impossible to long-jump 30 feet, but I don't listen to that kind of talk. Thoughts like that have a way of sinking into your feet."
Carl Lewis, who never achieved a 30ft (9.14m) long jump, but won the Olympic Games gold medal in the event in 1984, 1988, 1992 and 1996.

❋ THE WORLD'S FASTEST SPRINTER ❋

Donavan Bailey of Canada became the world's fastest man when he won the 100m gold medal at Atlanta in a new world record time of 9.84 seconds. The record has been broken a few times since Bailey won his gold, first by two Americans, Maurice Greene on 16 June 1999 (9.79secs) and Tim Montgomery on 14 September 2002 (9.78), and most recently by Jamaica's Asafa Powell, who set a blistering time of 9.74 seconds at Rieti, Italy, on 9 September 2005.

❋ GLOBAL UNITY DOWN UNDER ❋

Prior to the Melbourne Olympics of 1956, in the closing ceremony the athletes would march into the stadium by nation, just as they did in the opening ceremony. However, this protocol was set aside in Melbourne when John Ian Wing, a young Australian, suggested to the Australian IOC that the athletes enter the stadium for the closing ceremony together as a symbol of global unity. In his letter to the Australian NOC, Wing wrote: "During the Games there will be only one nation. War, politics and nationalities will be forgotten. What more could anybody want if the world could be made one nation."

❋ BRAVEHEART ❋

At the 1952 Games, Danish equestrian Lis Hartel won a silver medal in the dressage (held, like all the equestrian events, in Stockholm, Sweden). It was the first Olympics in which women competed against men in the event. What made Hartel's triumph truly amazing was that she had been paralysed by polio in 1944, and although she eventually managed to reactivate most of her muscles she remained paralysed below the knees. This keen horsewoman finished second in the Scandinavian Riding Championships to earn her place on Sweden's Olympic team for the 1952 Games. Hartel, who had to be helped on and off her horse, retained her silver medal four years later at the Melbourne Olympics.

❋ FANTASY WOMEN'S 100M OLYMPIC FINAL ❋

Lane No./Athlete   *Country*   *Olympic Medals*

1 Stanislawa Walasiewicz . Poland .... Gold – Los Angeles 1932, Silver – Berlin 1936
2 Wyomia Tyus .... USA .... 2 Gold – Tokyo 1964 & Mexico City 1968
3 Fanny Blankers-Koen . Netherlands .... Gold – London 1948
4 Renate Stecher .... E. Germany .... Gold – Munich 1972, Silver – Montreal 1976
5 Gail Devers .... USA .... 2 Gold – Barcelona 1992 & Atlanta 1996
6 Florence Griffith-Joyner . USA .... Gold – Seoul 1988
7 Evelyn Ashford .... USA .... Gold – Los Angeles 1984, Silver – Seoul 1988
8 Betty Cuthbert .... Australia .... Gold – Melbourne 1956

❋ JIM THORPE (1888–1953) ❋

Jacobus Franciscus ("Jim") Thorpe was born on 28 May 1888 in Bellemont, Oklahoma. Thorpe was raised as a Sac and Fox Indian under the native name Wa-Tho-Huk, meaning Bright Path. The story goes that Thorpe took up athletics at Carlisle in 1907 when he beat his school's best high jumper while still wearing his school clothes. In addition to athletic success at school Thorpe also excelled at American football, baseball, lacrosse and ballroom dancing. In 1911 Thorpe came to the attention of a football-mad American public when he scored all of his school's points in an 18–13 win over Harvard University. The versatile Thorpe played as defensive back, place-kicker, punter and running back for Carlisle's football team, and in 1912 he led them to the National Collegiate Championship.

In 1912, at the Stockholm Olympics, Thorpe represented the USA in two newly introduced events, the pentathlon and the decathlon. Thorpe dominated both events, claiming the gold medal in each. He also participated in the long jump and high jump, and on the very day that he won gold in the pentathlon he qualified for the high jump final, finishing fourth, and took seventh place in the long jump. During the closing ceremony of the Games he received two challenge prizes along with the two gold medals; the first was given to him by King Gustav V of Sweden for winning the decathlon, and the second by Czar Nicholas II of Russia for winning the pentathlon. When he returned to the USA he received a ticker-tape welcome in New York. However, in late January 1913, a few US newspapers published stories claiming that Thorpe had played professional baseball. In an open letter to the Amateur Athletic Union (AAU) Thorpe admitted that he had received payment to play professional baseball in 1909 and 1910. The AAU, unimpressed, immediately withdrew his amateur status and then wrote to the IOC asking them to do likewise. The IOC followed the AAU's lead and stripped him of his Olympic titles, medals and awards, and declared him to be a professional. However, he went on to have a highly successful career in American football, his first love, playing for the Canton Bulldogs, before becoming the first president of the National Football League (NFL). Thorpe also played Major League Baseball for the New York Giants, the Boston Braves and the Cincinnati Reds.

Did You Know That?

When King Gustav V of Sweden awarded Jim Thorpe his prize, saying, "You, sir, are the greatest athlete in the world," Thorpe is reported to have replied, "Thanks, King."

❊ THE WATER CUBE ❊

The Beijing National Aquatics Centre, also known as "The Water Cube" (or abbreviated $[H_2O]^3$) has been constructed alongside the National Stadium in the Olympic Forest Park. This showcase arena, staging the swimming, diving and synchronized swimming events at the 2008 Games, has an avant-garde structural design inspired by research done into the natural formation of soap bubbles. The water polo and the swimming discipline of the modern pentathlon were first planned to be held here too, but will be in the Ying Tung Natatorium.

❊ NAZI PROPAGANDA ❊

The German government saw the 1936 Olympics as the ideal opportunity to promote their Nazi ideology. The IOC commissioned Leni Riefenstahl, one of Hitler's favourite film-makers, to film the 1936 Games. Riefenstahl's film, entitled *Olympia*, and the techniques she employed have served as an inspiration to sports movie-makers ever since. Riefenstahl opted to highlight the aesthetics of the body by filming it from every angle.

❊ CROSS-CHANNEL SWIMMING GOLD ❊

At the Paris Games of 1924, US swimmer Gertrude Ederle won a gold medal in the 4x100m freestyle relay and bronze medals in the 100 metres and 400 metres freestyle. Two years later she caused a worldwide sensation by not only becoming the first woman to swim across the English Channel but also doing so in a time almost two hours faster than any man had ever achieved. Her historic and record-breaking cross-channel swim began at 7.05 a.m. on 6 August 1926 from Cap Gris-Nez, France, and 14 hours and 30 minutes later she came ashore at Kingsdown, England. Her record time was not beaten until 24 years later, when Florence Chadwick swam the channel in 13 hours, 20 minutes on 8 August 1950.

❊ TRIATHLON MAKES ITS OLYMPIC DEBUT ❊

The triathlon made its inaugural Olympic appearance in Sydney, set in the picturesque surroundings of the Sydney Opera House. Switzerland's Brigitte McMahon won the ladies' event, and then Canada's Simon Whitfield won the men's. A total of five nations made up the six medal places, with Switzerland claiming two of them thanks to Magali Messmer's bronze in the ladies' competition.

❋ THE GAMES OF THE V OLYMPIAD ❋

The 1912 Stockholm Olympics, the Games of the V Olympiad, were opened on 5 May 1912 by HRH King Gustav V. The most efficiently run Games to date, dubbed "The Swedish Masterpiece", the Stockholm Olympics witnessed the introduction of unofficial electronic timing devices for the track events, a photo-finish machine and the first use of a public address system. Also several new events were added to the Olympic programme in 1912, including the modern pentathlon, equestrian events and women's events in swimming and diving. A total of 28 nations sent 2,407 athletes (2,359 men, 48 women) to participate in 102 events across 14 sports. The closing ceremony took place on 27 July 1912.

Stockholm 1912 – Final Medals Table (Top 10)

Pos.	Nation	Gold	Silver	Bronze	Total
1	United States	25	19	19	63
2	Sweden	24	24	17	65
3	Great Britain	10	15	16	41
4	Finland	9	8	9	26
5	France	7	4	3	14
6	Germany	5	13	7	25
7	South Africa	4	2	0	6
8	Norway	4	1	4	9
9	Canada	3	2	3	8
	Hungary	3	2	3	8

❋ FIRST HOME TV GAMES ❋

London 1948 was the first Olympiad to be shown on home television, although the viewing figures were low. The reason for this is that very few people in Great Britain actually owned television sets.

❋ BACKING THE SOVIETS ❋

A total of 14 countries took part in the Soviet-led boycott of the 1984 Olympic Games:

Afghanistan ❖ Angola ❖ Bulgaria ❖ Cuba ❖ Czechoslovakia
East Germany ❖ Ethiopia ❖ Hungary ❖ Laos ❖ Mongolia
North Korea ❖ Poland ❖ USSR ❖ Vietnam

Iran and Libya also boycotted the Games, citing political reasons other than support for the Soviets.

❋ IOC PRESIDENTS FROM 1894 TO PRESENT ❋

Period	*Name*	*Country*
1894–96	Demetrius Vikelas	Greece
1896–1925	Baron Pierre de Coubertin	France
1925–42	Count Henri de Baillet-Latour	Belgium
1946–52	J. Sigfrid Edström	Sweden
1952–72	Avery Brundage	USA
1972–80	Lord Killanin	England
1980–2001	Juan Antonio Samaranch	Spain
2001–	Jacques Rogge	Belgium

❋ BIG RED MACHINE RULES THE POOL ❋

In the men's swimming competition in Barcelona, Russian swimmers dominated the freestyle events, winning the 50m, 100m, 200m, 400m and 4x200m relay. The two they failed to win were the 1500 metres, won by Australia's Kieren Perkins, and the 4x100m relay, which was claimed by the USA (Russia took the silver medal). Alexander Popov and Yevgeny Sadovyi won two gold medals each in individual events, while Sadovyi claimed a third in the 4x200m individual relay.

❋ ALL ON HER OWN ❋

Annegret Richter (West Germany), who won the women's 100m in Montreal 1976, was the only female athlete from outside Eastern Europe to win a gold medal on the track at the Games. East Germany's women won nine of the 14 track and field gold medals (with two going to the USSR and one each to Bulgaria and Poland) and made a clean sweep of the medal places in the pentathlon.

❋ POLITICAL GAMES DOWN UNDER ❋

In the lead-up to the 1956 Games, Australian politicians were divided over the cost to the country of hosting an Olympiad. The Premier of Victoria refused to allocate funds to build an Olympic Village in Melbourne, as there was a shortage of housing for the local population at the time. The Olympic Village was eventually constructed in Heidelberg West, a suburb of Melbourne. The Australian Prime Minister also stated that federal funds could not be used to pay for the costs of hosting the Games. IOC President Avery Brudage became so impatient with the political in-fighting that he almost awarded the 1956 Games to Rome instead.

✳ AN ACT OF SPORTSMANSHIP ✳

During the 1988 Games, Lawrence Lemieux (Canada) was sailing along in second place in the fifth of a seven-race Finn class and looking good to claim a silver medal when he abandoned the race to save two men. First he rescued Joseph Chan of Singapore and then sailed towards another Singapore sailor, Shaw Her Siew, who was clinging to his overturned boat. Lemieux waited for an official patrol boat to reach him and take the two sailors ashore before continuing in his event. However, he finished 22nd in the race, which ended his hopes of a medal. Shortly after the completion of the Finn class races the International Yacht Racing Union unanimously decided that Lemieux should be awarded second place in the fifth race, a decision none of the other contestants questioned. Although Lemieux did not win an Olympic medal, he was awarded the Pierre de Coubertin Medal for Sportsmanship. "By your sportsmanship, self-sacrifice and courage you embody all that is right with the Olympic ideal," said the IOC President Juan Antonio Samaranch.

✳ LONG'S LONG JUMP ADVICE ✳

At the Berlin Games of 1936 Jesse Owens, an African-American, won four gold medals, one of which was in the long jump event. Much to the dissatisfaction of the German officials, his German rival, Carl Ludwig "Lutz" Long, gave Owens advice on his technique after he almost failed to qualify for the final. Long had actually set a new Olympic record during his qualifying jump, but Owens bettered Long's distance in the final to claim the gold medal. Long was the first to congratulate Owens, and the pair walked arm in arm to the dressing-room. Following his death on 13 July 1943, Long was posthumously awarded the Pierre de Coubertin medal for sportsmanship. "It took a lot of courage for him to befriend me in front of Hitler," said Owens about Long's congratulations. "You can melt down all the medals and cups I have and they wouldn't be plating on the twenty-four kilates friendship that I felt for Lutz Long at that moment."

✳ OLYMPIC TALK (5) ✳

"The efficiency and almost mathematical precision with which the events were handled and the formal correctness of the arrangements made a great impression on me."
Avery Brundage, IOC President 1952–72, describing the 1912 Stockholm Olympics

❋ OLYMPIC MASCOTS ❋

The Mexico City Olympics of 1968 was the first time the IOC introduced an official mascot for the Summer Olympics. Since then each Olympiad has had its mascot:

1968 Mexico City
An unnamed red jaguar.

1972 Munich
Waldi, a dachshund dog, chosen to represent the attributes required for athletes – Resistance, Tenacity and Agility.
Designer: Otl Aicher.

1976 Montreal
Amik, a beaver, one of Canada's national symbols.

1980 Moscow
Misha, a bear cub, designed by children's books illustrator Victor Chizhikov.

1984 Los Angeles
Sam the Eagle, a bald eagle, one of the symbols of the USA, designed by Robert Moore from the Walt Disney Company.

1988 Seoul
Hodori and Hosuni, two tigers (Hodori is a male cub, Hosuni female), two of Korea's legends. Designer: Hyum Kim.

1992 Barcelona
Cobi, a Cubist Catalan sheepdog. Designer: Javier Marischal.

1996 Atlanta
Izzy, an abstract figure whose name was changed from Whatizit (i.e. What is it?).

2000 Sydney
Olly, a kookaburra, representing the Olympic spirit of generosity. Olly's name derives from Olympic.
Syd, a platypus, representing the environment and the energy of the people of Australia. Syd's name derives from Sydney.
Millie, an echidna representing the millennium.

2004 Athens
Athena and Phevos, brother and sister, two modern children resembling ancient Greek dolls. Designer: Spyros Gogos.

2008 Beijing
The *Fuwa*, comprising of five figures: *Beibei*, with a fish design, *Jingjing*, with a giant panda and lotus design, *Huanhuan*, the Olympic Flame, *Yingying*, with a Tibetan antelope design and *Nini*, with a swallow design. Together the five names form the Chinese phrase *"Beijing huan ying ni"*, which translated means "Beijing welcomes you". Designer: Han Meilin.

✳ BLACK POWER SALUTE ✳

In the final of the 200 metres in Mexico City, Tommie Smith of the USA won the gold medal, Peter Norman of Australia the silver and Smith's team-mate, John Carlos, the bronze. Smith won the race in a new world record time for 200 metres of 19.83 seconds. However, it was the medal ceremony that followed which stands out as one of the most defining moments in the history of the modern Olympics. Both Smith and Carlos walked on to the podium shoeless (they wore black socks to represent black poverty) and when "The Star Spangled Banner" (the US national anthem) was played they both bowed their heads and gave the Black Power salute. Smith and Carlos made the gesture to protest at the blatant discrimination against blacks in America. All three athletes on the podium wore OPHR (Olympic Project for Human Rights) badges, while Smith also wore a black scarf around his neck and Carlos a set of black beads. It was Norman in fact who suggested that Smith and Carlos wear one black glove each when it emerged that Carlos had forgotten his pair – Smith wore the right glove and Carlos the left. A number of IOC officials, most notably the President, Avery Brundage, believed that their protest was a political statement which had no place at an Olympiad. Both Smith and Carlos were thrown off the US team by the United States Olympic Committee (USOC) and banned from the Olympic Village. They also received lifetime Olympic bans. However, many people praised the two athletes for their bravery in taking a stance against racism in the USA, and Germany's Martin Jellinghaus, winner of the bronze medal in the 4x400m relay, wore an OPHR badge in support of Smith and Carlos. Interviewed after the most famous civil rights protest in Olympic history, Smith said: "If I win, I am American, not a black American. But if I did something bad, then they would say I am a Negro. We are black and we are proud of being black. Black America will understand what we did tonight."

✳ PERUVIAN WITHDRAWAL ✳

Peru beat Austria 4–2 after extra time in the quarter-finals of the football tournament at the Berlin Games. However, a rematch was ordered when the Austrians claimed that the pitch was too small for competitive football matches and that the Peruvian fans had stormed the field after the fourth goal was scored. The Peruvian government regarded this as an insult and ordered their Olympic team to withdraw in protest. The Austrians went through, but Italy won the gold medal with Austria taking silver and Norway bronze.

❊ GRECO-ROMAN HAT-TRICK ❊

Swedish wrestler Carl Westergren won his third Greco-Roman title during the 1932 Los Angeles Olympics when he claimed gold in the heavyweight (+87kg) division. Amazingly, he won his three gold medals in three different divisions. In 1920 (Antwerp) he won the middleweight (67.5–75kg) gold, and in 1924 (Paris) he won gold in the light heavyweight (75–82.5kg) event. Meanwhile Westergren's compatriot Ivar Johansson, a Swedish policeman, won gold medals in both freestyle (middleweight, 72–79kg) and Greco-Roman wrestling (welterweight, 66–72kg) at the 1932 Games.

❊ ST LOUIS MIRRORS PARIS FARCE ❊

Just as the events at the Paris Olympics of 1900 were relegated to sideshow activities in comparison to the events forming the 1900 World's Fair held at the same time in Paris, St Louis followed a similar farcical path. Like the Paris Games, the St Louis Games were held over a period of five months, and James Edward Sullivan, principal organizer of the 1904 Olympics, even attempted to hold an event every day for the duration of the fair. The 1904 Olympic events were once again intertwined with other sporting events, but unlike 1900, when the term "Olympic" was rarely used to describe an event, Sullivan gave all his events the Olympic label. In a number of the events, the US National Championship was combined with the Olympic Championship because there were no competitors from other nations to compete in the sport. Indeed, of the 651 athletes 525 were American, and only 42 of the 91 events included any athletes who were not from the USA.

❊ SRI LANKAN FIRST ❊

At the Sydney Olympics Susanthika Jayasinghe became the first Sri Lankan woman to win an Olympic medal when she took the bronze in the 200 metres.

❊ FIRST OLYMPIC CHAMPION IN 1,503 YEARS ❊

On the opening day of the Games, 6 April 1896, James Connolly of the USA won the triple jump to become the first Olympic champion in 1,503 years. Connolly also finished second in the high jump and third in the long jump. He went on to participate in the Paris Olympics of 1900, where he claimed a second bronze medal.

THE GAMES OF THE VII OLYMPIAD

The 1920 Olympics at Antwerp, in Belgium, were officially opened on 20 April 1920 by His Majesty King Albert. The previous scheduled Games – those of the VI Olympiad – were originally to have taken place in Berlin in 1916, but the First World War prevented this from happening. The IOC awarded the next Games to Belgium to pay tribute to the suffering endured by the Belgian people during the war (the VI Olympiad was the first lost Olympiad). The 1920 Games witnessed two milestones in the history of the Olympics: the Olympic flag (created by Baron de Coubertin), with the five rings signifying the union of five continents, was first flown there; and the Olympic oath was first spoken there by Victor Boin, who represented the host nation in fencing and water polo. The outstanding star of the Games was unquestionably Italy's Nedo Nadi, who claimed five of the six gold medals on offer in the fencing events. Oscar Swahan, a Swedish shooter aged 72, won a silver medal in the team double-shot running deer event to become the oldest Olympic medallist ever. On her way to winning the gold medal in all three women's swimming contests, Ethelda Bleibtrey of the USA swam in five races, including preliminary heats, and broke the world record in every one. A total of 29 nations sent 2,626 athletes (2,561 men, 65 women) to participate in 154 events across 22 sports. The closing ceremony took place on 12 September 1920.

Antwerp 1920 – Final Medals Table (Top 10)

Pos.	*Nation*	*Gold*	*Silver*	*Bronze*	*Total*
1	United States	41	27	27	95
2	Sweden	19	18	24	61
3	Great Britain	15	15	13	43
4	Finland	15	10	9	34
5	Belgium	14	11	11	36
6	Norway	13	9	9	31
7	Italy	13	5	5	23
8	France	9	19	13	41
9	Netherlands	4	2	5	11
10	Denmark	3	9	1	13

TOUR DE FRANCE WINNER CLAIMS GOLD

At Atlanta 1996, professional cyclists were admitted to an Olympiad for the first time. Spain's Miguel Indurain, five times winner of the Tour de France, triumphed in the inaugural individual time trial event.

❊ THE FOSBURY FLOP ❊

Richard "Dick" Fosbury won the high jump gold medal in Mexico City with his innovative "Fosbury Flop" technique, setting a new Olympic record of 2.24 metres (7 feet, 4¼ inches). Whereas most high jumpers practised the Californian western roll, Fosbury's method was to sprint diagonally towards the bar and then curve and leap backwards over it. After the Games the Californian western roll was a thing of the past.

❊ SUMMON THE HEROES ❊

The official theme music of the Olympiad was "Summon the Heroes" written by John Williams, his third composition at an Olympiad. However, the official song of the 1996 Olympics was "Reach", sung by Gloria Estefan.

❊ DOUBLE DOUBLE EAST GERMAN GOLD ❊

At the 1980 Olympics Waldemar Cierpinski of East Germany retained his Olympic marathon gold medal, while his compatriot Barbel Wockel won the 200m gold to become the first female athlete to successfully defend this title.

❊ MALE WINS WOMEN'S 100M GOLD ❊

Stanislawa Walasiewicz from Poland won the 100m gold medal at the Los Angeles Games of 1932. The 21-year-old Pole equalled the world record of 11.9 seconds in her heat and then recorded the same blistering time in the final. Later the same day she finished sixth in the discus throw. When she returned to Poland a huge number of fans turned out to greet her arrival in the port of Gdynia, and a few days later she was presented with the Golden "Cross of Merit", a medal awarded in recognition of services to the State. Four years later she claimed the silver medal in the same event in Berlin. Walasiewicz later moved to America and took the name Stella Walsh. Following her death on 4 December 1980, killed as an innocent bystander in an armed robbery, an autopsy on her body revealed that she possessed male genitalia. Subsequently there were calls for all of her achievements and records to be stricken from the record books but this was something neither the IOC nor the IAAF implemented. During her career, Walasiewicz set over 100 national and world records, including 51 Polish records, 18 world records and eight European records.

※ JAMES BOND IN THE SYDNEY OLYMPICS ※

In the James Bond film *Die Another Day*, Verity (played by Madonna) claims that the Miranda Frost character won a gold medal in fencing at the Olympic Games in Sydney.

※ THE ROY JONES CONTROVERSY ※

In the final of the light-middleweight boxing division (up to 71kg) at the 1988 Olympics the red-hot favourite to win the gold medal, Roy Jones Jr of the USA, was beaten by the home favourite, Park Si-Hun of South Korea. Jones controversially lost the fight 3–2, leading to allegations that South Korean officials had rigged the judging, with many hailing Jones as the true Olympic champion. Indeed, in the fight Jones absolutely battered his opponent over the three rounds, landing 86 punches to Park's 32, and was awarded the Val Barker trophy as the best stylistic boxer of the 1988 Games. Shortly after the fight ended one of the judges admitted that the decision was a mistake, and all three judges who voted for Si-Hun were subsequently suspended. Nine years later the IOC published the official report into the incident, in which it was revealed that three of the judges were wined and dined by South Korean officials. However, it was nine years too late for Jones, and surprisingly the IOC did not overturn the result. The incident, coupled with another hotly disputed decision awarded in favour of Ivailo Marinov (Bulgaria) against the USA's Michael Carbajal in the light-flyweight event (up to 48 kg) at the same Olympics, resulted in the IOC creating a new scoring system for Olympic boxing.

※ HONG KONG GOLD ※

Lee Lai Shan made history at Atlanta by winning Hong Kong's first, and to date only, gold medal when she won the sailboard (Mistral) event.

※ BROTHERS ABRAHAMS ※

Sidney Solomon "Solly" Abrahams competed in the Intercalated Games held in Athens in 1906, finishing fifth in the long jump. At the 1912 Stockholm Olympics he finished in 11th place in the same event. Abrahams served as Chief Justice of Ceylon from 1936 to 1939. Solly was the older brother of the famed Olympian Harold Abrahams, who won the 100m gold medal at the 1924 Paris Olympics.

❇ OLYMPIC TALK (6) ❇

"Such is the power of a good 'story' that for every thousand people who know Dorando's name, not even one is probably able to say who officially won the London marathon."
Harold Abrahams, 1924 gold medallist, speaking about Dorando Pietri in the 1908 Olympic marathon in London

❇ CUBAN RING MASTERS ❇

In the 1980 boxing competitions Cuba won six gold, two silver and two bronze medals from the 11 weight divisions. The only division in which they missed out on a podium place was flyweight. This impressive haul equalled the Olympic record, which had stood since St Louis 1904, when the USA won 11 boxing medals on home soil. The Cubans' achievement was in fact considerably greater, because in 1904 there were few contestants from outside the USA.

❇ SEVEN INTO TEN ❇

Romania's Nadia Comaneci recorded seven perfect scores of 10.00 in gymnastics at the 1976 Olympics. However, as no gymnast had ever reached the magical figure before, and the scoreboard could actually display only three digits, her maximum marks were shown as 1.00.

❇ FIRST FEMALE ATHLETES ❇

Madame Brohy and Mademoiselle Ohnier were the first women to participate in the Olympic Games when they represented France at croquet at the Paris Olympics of 1900.

❇ JUMPING TO GLORY ❇

At the Tokyo Olympics Mary Rand became the first ever British female athlete to win an Olympic gold medal in a track and field event when she won the long jump final. She won the gold medal with a new world record leap of 6.76 metres, and today a plaque can be found in the Market Place of her home town, Wells, Somerset, commemorating her achievement. In Tokyo she also won a silver medal in the pentathlon and a bronze medal in the 4x100m relay. In 1964 she won the BBC Sports Personality of the Year Award, and in 1965 was awarded an MBE.

✳ FANTASY MEN'S 200M OLYMPIC FINAL ✳

Lane No./Athlete	Country	Olympic Medals
1 Jesse Owens	USA	Gold – Berlin 1936
2 Pietro Mennea	Italy	Gold – Moscow 1980
3 Carl Lewis	USA	Gold – Los Angeles 1984, Silver – Seoul 1988
4 Konstantinos Kenteris	Greece	Gold – Sydney 2000
5 Michael Johnson	USA	Gold – Atlanta 1996
6 Bobby Kerr	Canada	Gold – London 1908
7 Don Quarrie	Jamaica	Gold – Montreal 1976
8 Andy Stanfield	USA	Gold – Helsinki 1952, Silver – Melbourne 1956

❋ JOHNNY WEISSMULLER – FILMOGRAPHY ❋

Johnny Weissmuller, who won five Olympic swimming gold medals in 1924 and 1928, starred in many Hollywood movies after retiring:

Film	Part played
Glorifying the American Girl (1929) (Paramount)	Adonis
Crystal Champions (1929) (Paramount)	Himself
Tarzan the Ape Man (1932) (MGM)	Tarzan
Tarzan and His Mate (1934) (MGM	Tarzan
Tarzan Escapes (1936) (MGM)	Tarzan
Tarzan Finds a Son! (1939) (MGM)	Tarzan
Tarzan's Secret Treasure (1941) (MGM)	Tarzan
Tarzan's New York Adventure (1942) (MGM)	Tarzan
Tarzan Triumphs (1943) (RKO Pathé)	Tarzan
Tarzan's Desert Mystery (1943) (RKO Pathé)	Tarzan
Stage Door Canteen (1943) (United Artists)	Himself
Tarzan and the Amazons (1945) (RKO Pathé)	Tarzan
Swamp Fire (1946) (Paramount)	Johnny Duval
Tarzan and the Leopard Woman (1946) (RKO Pathé)	Tarzan
Tarzan and the Huntress (1947) (RKO Pathé)	Tarzan
Tarzan and the Mermaids (1948) (RKO Pathé)	Tarzan
Jungle Jim (1948) (Columbia)	Jungle Jim
The Lost Tribe (1949) (Columbia)	Jungle Jim
Mark of the Gorilla (1950) (Columbia)	Jungle Jim
Captive Girl (1950) (Columbia)	Jungle Jim
Pypmy Island (1950) (Columbia)	Jungle Jim
Fury of the Congo (1951) (Columbia)	Jungle Jim
Jungle Manhunt (1951) (Columbia)	Jungle Jim
Jungle Jim in the Forbidden Land (1952) (Columbia)	Jungle Jim
Voodoo Tiger (1952) (Columbia)	Jungle Jim
Savage Mutiny (1953) (Columbia)	Jungle Jim
Valley of Head Hunters (1953) (Columbia)	Jungle Jim
Killer Ape (1953) (Columbia)	Jungle Jim
Jungle Man-Eaters (1954) (Columbia)	Jungle Jim
Cannibal Attack (1954) (Columbia)	Himself
Jungle Moon Men (1955) (Columbia)	Himself
Devil Goddess (1955) (Columbia)	Himself
The Phynx (1970) (Warner Bros.)	Cameo
Won Ton Ton, the Dog Who Saved Hollywood (1976) (Paramount)	Crewman

Did You Know That?
Johnny Weissmuller has a star on the Hollywood Walk of Fame.

✻ THE GAMES OF THE VIII OLYMPIAD ✻

The 1924 Paris Olympics were officially opened by President Gaston Doumergue of France on 4 May 1924 at the Stade Olympique Yves-du-Manoir. It was at the 1924 Paris Olympiad that the Olympic Motto, Citius, Altius, Fortius ("Faster, Higher, Stronger"), was introduced. These Games also witnessed the inaugural closing ceremony tradition of raising three flags: those of the International Olympic Committee, the host nation and the next host nation. Johnny Weissmuller of the USA won three swimming gold medals, in the 100m freestyle, the 400m freestyle and the 4x200m freestyle, plus a bronze medal in the men's water polo. He later won two more gold medals at the 1928 Olympics in Amsterdam and went on to stardom playing Tarzan in 12 Hollywood movies. The 1924 Games witnessed the introduction of women's fencing, with Denmark's Ellen Osiier taking the gold medal without losing a single bout. Finland's Paavo Nurmi won five gold medals to add to the three he had won in Antwerp in 1920. In total some 1,000 journalists covered the events as the Games began to attract global attention. A total of 44 nations sent 3,089 athletes (2,954 men, 135 women) to participate in 126 events across 17 sports. The closing ceremony took place on 27 July 1924.

Paris 1924 – Final Medals Table (Top 10)

Pos.	Nation	Gold	Silver	Bronze	Total
1	USA	45	27	27	99
2	Finland	14	13	10	37
3	France	13	15	10	38
4	Great Britain	9	13	12	34
5	Italy	8	3	5	16
6	Switzerland	7	8	10	25
7	Norway	5	2	3	10
8	Sweden	4	13	12	29
9	Netherlands	4	1	5	10
10	Belgium	3	7	3	13

✻ TRIPLE GENERATION MEDAL WINNERS ✻

Andreas Keller won a gold medal with the Unified Germany team in field hockey at the 1992 Olympics. He became the third generation of his family to win a medal in the event, his grandfather, Erwin, having won a silver medal at Berlin 1936 and his father, Carsten, a gold medal, again on home soil at Munich 1972.

❋ INAUGURAL MEDALS ❋

At the 1896 Athens Olympics winners were awarded a silver medal, an olive branch and a diploma. The athletes who finished second were presented with a copper medal, a branch of laurel and a diploma. On the front of the medal the face of Zeus, the Greek god, was depicted along with his hand holding a globe with the winged victory on it and the caption "Olympia", written in Greek. The back of each medal had the Acropolis site with the words "International Olympic Games in Athens in 1896", also written in Greek.

❋ LONDON SPAWNS THE IAAF ❋

The 1908 London Olympics prompted the establishment of standard rules for sports, as well as the selection of judges from different countries, instead of only the host nation, to officiate at the Games. The controversial 400 metres final also resulted in the formation of the International Amateur Athletics Federation, the purpose of which was to set uniform worldwide rules for athletics.

❋ DALEY'S DOUBLE GOLD ❋

In Los Angeles Daley Thompson (GB) once again found himself up against his old foe and nemesis, Jurgen Hingsen of West Germany, in the decathlon. The two super-fit athletes were neck and neck after the first seven events, but then Daley kicked into top gear and pulled away from Hingsen with superb performances in the pole vault and the javelin throw to retain his Olympic title. Having already secured the gold medal, Thompson then set his sights on breaking Hingsen's world record score of 8,832 points. The double Olympic champion needed to run the final event, the 1500 metres, in a time of 4:34.58 or better to break Hingsen's world record, but clocked 4:35.00, having appeared to ease up at the finishing line. Daley won the gold medal with a score of 8,798 points, while Hingsen claimed the silver medal with 8,673 points and West Germany's Siegfried Wentz the bronze with 8,412. In 1985, however, IAAF officials re-examined the photo timer results at the 1984 Olympics and found that Thompson had clocked a time of 14.33 seconds in the 110m hurdles, as opposed to the 14.34 seconds he was originally given, making his overall score 8,847 points, a new world record. The engaging if controversial Daley won the BBC Sports Personality of the Year award in 1982, and was awarded the OBE in 1983, followed by a CBE in 2000.

�֍ PAAVO NURMI (1897–1973) ✷

Paavo Johannes Nurmi was born on 13 June 1897 in Turku, Finland, and was one of the greatest middle- and long-distance runners who ever lived. Nurmi was a class above his peers and ahead of his time in his training methods, never racing without a stopwatch in his hand. Nurmi was an introvert and disliked publicity, but during the 1920s, he played an important part in helping Finland establish itself on the world stage following its independence from Russia.

Nurmi burst on to the world stage in 1920 at the Olympic Games held in Antwerp, Belgium. The 23-year-old Finn won gold medals in the 8,000 and 10,000 metres cross-country events, claimed a third gold medal in the team cross-country race, and won a silver medal in the 5,000 metres. Nurmi's haul of medals helped Finland break the USA's dominance in track and field and to a total of nine medals at the Games. During the 1924 Paris Olympics, Nurmi won five gold medals, winning the 1500 metres, the 5,000 metres and the 3,000m team race and retaining the two cross-country events he won in 1920. Nurmi only had 26 minutes' rest between the 1500m and 5,000m races. The 1924 Olympics was the last time an Olympiad featured cross-country events: in one race the heat had forced over half of the runners to drop out, with many ending up in hospital. Fearing for his health, the Finnish Olympic team officials refused to enter Nurmi for the 10,000m event. Nurmi was furious, and when he returned to Finland after the Games he embarrassed the same officials by setting an emphatic world record in the 10,000 metres. Nurmi ended his Olympic career at the 1928 Olympics in Amsterdam, winning gold in the 10,000 metres and silver in the 5,000 metres and the 3,000 metres steeplechase.

Nurmi was not allowed to compete in the 1932 Olympics, as he was classed as a professional. The main instigators behind Nurmi's ban from these Games were Sweden, and in particular Sigfrid Edstrom, President of the International Amateur Athletics Federation (IAAF) and Vice-President of the International Olympic Committee (IOC). Despite pleas from his fellow athletes for Nurmi to be allowed to race in the 1932 marathon, he was not. A proud Finn, Nurmi won a total of nine gold and three silver medals at three Olympiads (1920, 1924 & 1928). In 1952 he was given the honour of lighting the Olympic flame for the Summer Olympics held in Helsinki. He died in 1973.

Did You Know That?
A statue of Paavo Nurmi stands in front of the Olympic Stadium in Helsinki.

❋ OLYMPIC TALK (7) ❋

"Success in sport as in almost anything comes from devotion. The athlete must make a devotion of his specialty."
Hudson Strode's** description of **Paavo Nurmi

❋ DRUG TESTS INTRODUCED ❋

Knud Jenson, a Danish cyclist, died from a drug overdose during the road race at the Rome Games. His death shocked the IOC and cycling's governing body, the International Cycling Federation, which became the first international body to introduce drug tests.

❋ THE FIRST FOOTBALL WORLD CUP ❋

At the 1928 Olympics in Amsterdam, Uruguay retained its Olympic title, beating South American rivals Argentina 1–0 in a replay after the first match ended 1–1. Both nations reached the final with relative ease. Uruguay beat the host nation, the Netherlands, 2–0 in the round of the last 16 and followed this with a 4–1 win over Germany in the quarter-finals and a 3–2 victory over Italy in the semi-finals. Argentina hammered the USA 11–2 in the last-16 round, beat Belgium 6–3 in the quarter-finals and thrashed Egypt 6–0 in the semi-finals. The attractiveness of an all-South American final created enormous interest, and not just with the football-mad Dutch public, 250,000 requests for tickets coming in from all over Europe. Uruguay's Scarone scored the winning goal in the replay of the final, while Uruguay's double gold achievement was recognized the following year when the FIFA Congress, held in Barcelona, awarded the Uruguayans the honour of playing host to the inaugural FIFA World Cup Finals in 1930. Uruguay was crowned FIFA World Cup Champions on 30 July 1930 after defeating Argentina 4–2 in the final played in Montevideo. Up to 1928, the Olympic football tournament was regarded as the "football world championship". In fact the Olympic tournaments of 1920 (with 14 participating nations), 1924 (with 22) and 1928 (17) all had a greater number of participants than the first World Cup, in 1930, which had 13.

❋ GREEK TRIUMPH ❋

Fencer Leonidas Pyrgos became Greece's first modern Olympic champion by winning the masters foil competition at the Athens Games in 1896.

❊ McDONALD'S AT THE OLYMPICS ❊

In the lead-up to the 1984 Games the McDonald's fast food giant ran a promotion whereby they gave every customer who purchased a meal deal a scratch-card. Each card revealed the name of an Olympic event, with the promise that if the USA won a gold medal in that event the customer would win a free item from their menu. When the Soviets led a 14-nation boycott of the Games, only withdrawing two months before they were held, McDonald's reportedly lost millions of dollars as the USA won 83 gold medals. This incident was parodied in the hit cartoon television series *The Simpsons* in the episode entitled "Lisa's Final Word". Krusty the Clown decides to run a promotion in his fast food store, where the Krusty Burger is named as the "Official Meat-Flavoured Sandwich of the 1984 Olympics". The same principle applied, with scratch-cards being handed out with the promise that if the USA won the event then the customer would win a free Krusty Burger. However, Krusty rigged the competition by putting on the scratch-cards only those events that were usually dominated by communist bloc countries. When the Soviet-led boycott of the Games took place, Krusty lost over $40 million.

❊ BIRD'S NEST HOSTS THE WORLD ❊

The track and field events at the 2008 Olympic Games will be held in Beijing National Stadium. Known as "The Bird's Nest", because of its highly distinctive twig-like structural elements and bowl-shaped roof, it will seat 100,000 spectators for the Games but will then be reduced to a capacity of 80,000. Built on the Olympic Green in Beijing, it was designed by the Pritzker Prize-winning Swiss architects Jacques Herzog and Pierre de Meuron – designers of London's Tate Modern gallery – while Ai Weiwei, a contemporary Chinese artist, was the project's artistic consultant. The stadium cost 3.5 billion Chinese yuan (£215m) to build.

❊ FULFILLING HIGH EXPECTATIONS ❊

Dutch cyclist Leontien van Moorsel lived up to the huge billing she was given in the lead-up to the 2000 Olympics by winning three gold medals and one silver medal. She won the road race, the time trial and the individual pursuit and claimed a silver medal in the points race. Four years later in Athens she retained her time trial Olympic crown and won a bronze medal in the individual pursuit. During her career van Moorsel (whose married name is Leontien Zijlaard-van Moorsel) also won four track World Championships gold medals and four road World Championships gold medals.

✳ PAKISTAN END INDIAN RULE ✳

In the men's field hockey competition during the 1960 Games, Pakistan prevented their bitter rivals, India, from claiming a seventh consecutive gold medal in the event. India had won the previous six Olympic titles, dating back to the 1928 Games, but had to settle for silver on this occasion, with Spain winning the bronze. It was also the first ever gold medal won by Pakistan at an Olympiad.

✳ GOLD MEDAL IN THREE CLASSES ✳

Soviet sailor Valentyn Mankin won the gold medal in the Finn class at the 1968 Mexico City Olympics. Four years later in Munich he entered the Tempest class and won gold with Vitaly Dyrdyra. At the 1976 Olympics in Montreal he claimed a silver medal in the Tempest class alongside a new partner, Vladyslav Akimenko. When the 1980 Olympics were held in his native Russia, the 41-year-old Mankin teamed up with Aleksandrs Muzichenko and entered the Star class. Remarkably Mankin and Muzichenko claimed the gold medal in the final race, making Mankin the only sailor in Olympic history to win gold medals in three different classes.

✳ WHO'S THE GRANDDADDY? ✳

At the Games of 1908, Sweden's shooter Oscar Swahn won two gold medals in the running deer, single shot events (individual and team). He also won a bronze medal in the running deer double shot individual event. Swahn was 60 years old during the 1908 Games and a year younger than Britain's Joshua Kearney "Jerry" Miller, who claimed gold in the free rifle at 1,000 yards in 1908. Miller was 61 years and four days old when he won his gold medal. In 1912, on home ground at the Stockholm Olympics, Swahn was again a member of the single shot running deer team which won the gold medal. He also secured a second successive bronze in the individual double shot running deer event. At 64 years old he became the oldest Olympic gold medallist ever, a record that still stands today. Finally, aged 72, he was the oldest competitor at the 1920 Olympics held in Antwerp, Belgium, where he managed a fourth place finish in the team single shot running deer event and a silver medal in the team double shot running deer competition. His silver medal made him the oldest Olympic medallist of any colour of all time (excluding the art competitions). He was 72 years and 279 days old. Sadly, illness prevented the 76-year-old Swahn from participating in the 1924 Olympics.

✳ THE GAMES OF THE IX OLYMPIAD ✳

The 1928 Amsterdam Olympics were officially opened on 17 May 1928 by His Royal Highness Prince Hendrik. At the opening ceremony the Greek athletes led the Parade of Nations, with the host nation, the Netherlands, marching into the Olympisch Stadion last. Thus a new Olympic protocol was established: Greece first, hosts last. Henri Denis, a Dutch footballer, pronounced the Olympic oath. The Amsterdam Games saw the number of female athletes more than double, the IOC having finally permitted women to enter gymnastics and athletics. The 1928 Games saw Asian athletes winning gold medals for the first time: Japan's Mikio Oda won the triple jump (Asia's first Olympic champion in an individual event), and his fellow countryman, Yoshiyuki Tsuruta, won the 200 metres breaststroke. In the field hockey tournament (men's) India claimed the gold medal to begin a dominance of the sport at the Games, winning six consecutive gold medals between 1928 and 1956. However, not to be outdone, Hungary began their own impressive winning streak by claiming the first of seven consecutive Olympic gold medals in team sabre fencing. A total of 46 nations sent 2,883 athletes (2,606 men, 277 women) to participate in 109 events across 14 sports. The closing ceremony took place on 28 August 1928. Los Angeles (USA) and Rome had also expressed an interest in hosting the 1928 Games. Amsterdam's successful bid followed unsuccessful ones for both the 1920 and 1924 Olympiads.

Amsterdam 1928 – Final Medals Table (Top 10)

Pos.	Nation	Gold	Silver	Bronze	Total
1	USA	22	18	16	56
2	Germany	10	7	14	31
3	Finland	8	8	9	25
4	Sweden	7	6	12	25
5	Italy	7	5	7	19
6	Switzerland	7	4	4	15
7	France	6	10	5	21
8	Netherlands	6	9	4	19
9	Hungary	4	5	0	9
10	Canada	4	4	7	15

✳ IOC CALLS FOR A TRUCE ✳

At Barcelona in 1992, for the first time in Olympic history, the International Olympic Committee launched an appeal for the observance of the Olympic Truce.

❋ COMANECI CLAIMS TRIPLE GOLD ❋

Romania's Nadia Comaneci, winner of five Olympic gold medals in gymnastics, took up the sport at the age of six after the Romanian coach Bela Karolyi noticed Nadia and a friend turning cartwheels in a schoolyard. At the 1976 Olympics in Montreal, 14-year-old Nadia won three gold medals (all-around, balance beam and uneven bars), a silver medal (team competition) and a bronze medal (floor exercise). Comaneci was the first Romanian gymnast to win the all-around title at an Olympiad and she also holds the record as the youngest ever all-around Olympic gymnastics champion. Indeed, the latter record will never be broken as gymnasts must now be 16 years of age instead of 15 in the calendar year to compete in the Olympic Games. In 1980, at the Moscow Olympics, Nadia successfully defended her Olympic title in the balance beam and tied with Nellie Kim (USSR) for the gold medal in the floor exercise, her fifth Olympic gold medal. At the Moscow Games she also claimed a silver medal in the all-around competition and a silver medal in the team competition.

❋ THE MOST FAMOUS LOSING OLYMPIAN ❋

Dorando Pietri "won" the marathon of the London Olympics in 1908 but after the race was disqualified because officials had to help the dazed and confused Italian across the finish line. Indeed, 10 minutes of his "winning" time of 2 hours, 54 minutes and 46 seconds were required to assist him over the final 350 metres of the marathon. "I am not the marathon winner. Instead, as the English say, I am the one who won and lost victory" – Dorando Pietri, quoted in the *Corriere della Sera* on 30 July 1908.

❋ ONE LEG, SIX MEDALS ❋

George Eyser of the USA won six medals at St Louis in 1904: three gold (men's artistic gymnastics, vault & parallel bars), two silver (combined four events & pommelhorse) and one bronze (horizontal bar). Amazingly, Eyser won his medals with a wooden leg, having lost a leg after being run over by a train.

❋ FALLEN RUNNER ❋

Francisco Lazaro of Portugal collapsed from dehydration during the marathon in 1912 in Stockholm and died the next day at the Serafimer Hospital of heat exhaustion.

❋ THE BIG KAHUNA ❋

Duke Paoa Kahinu Mokoe Hulikohola Kahanamoku, nicknamed "The Big Kahuna", had won the gold medal in the 100 metres freestyle swimming event at the 1912 Olympics in Stockholm. The Games of 1916 were cancelled because of the First World War, but in 1920 Duke retained his Olympic 100m freestyle championship in Antwerp. Prior to the 1912 Stockholm Olympics Duke participated in an amateur swimming event in Honolulu Harbor on 11 August 1911, and swam the 100 metres freestyle in a time of 55.4 seconds, beating the existing world record by 4.6 seconds. When his time was sent to Amateur Athletic Union officials in New York the AAU replied: "Unacceptable. No one swims this fast. Hawaiian judges alerted to use stop watches, not alarm clocks!"

❋ DOWN UNDER ON TOP ❋

During the 1956 Olympics the Australian swimmers cleaned up in the pool. They won all of the freestyle races, men's and women's, and claimed a total of 14 medals (eight gold, four silver and two bronze) from the 13 swimming events in one of the most dominant team displays ever witnessed at an Olympiad. The USA team were the next most successful with 11 medals. In both the men's and women's 100m freestyle events, Australian swimmers occupied the first three places, and the hosts also won both team relay races. Meanwhile, Murray Rose (Australia) became the first male swimmer to win two freestyle events (400m & 1500m) since Johnny Weissmuller (USA) in 1924, and Dawn Fraser (Australia) won gold medals in the 100 metres freestyle and as the lead-off swimmer on the 4x100m relay team.

❋ SPEED MACHINE ❋

Great Britain's Chris Boardman won the 4,000m individual track pursuit gold medal at the 1992 Games, riding a revolutionary new "super bike". Four years later he elected not to defend his Olympic title and opted for the 52km time trial, winning the bronze medal at the 1996 Atlanta Games. Chris became so famous after winning gold in Barcelona that he appeared on television quite regularly during the 1990s. During an episode of the popular comedy *Only Fools and Horses*, Del Boy, played by David Jason, is at his pitch in the market attempting to flog some dodgy cycling helmets. At one point he shouts out to the passing shoppers: "Cycling helmets, as worn by Chris Boardman, and by his brother Stan Boardman."

❋ OLYMPIC TALK (8) ❋

"As long as Morceli (Noureddine Morceli) is in the race, it is always a race for second place."
Venuste Niyongabo, Burundi athlete, 1996 Games

❋ MODERN SUMMER OLYMPIC GAMES HOSTS ❋

Year	Host City/Nation
1896	Athens, Greece
1900	Paris, France
1904	St Louis, USA
1908	London, England
1912	Stockholm, Sweden
1920	Antwerp, Belgium
1924	Paris, France
1928	Amsterdam, the Netherlands
1932	Los Angeles, USA
1936	Berlin, Germany
1948	London, England
1952	Helsinki, Finland
1956	Melbourne, Australia
1960	Rome, Italy
1964	Tokyo, Japan
1968	Mexico City, Mexico
1972	Munich, West Germany
1976	Montreal, Canada
1980	Moscow, USSR
1984	Los Angeles, USA
1988	Seoul, South Korea
1992	Barcelona, Spain
1996	Atlanta, USA
2000	Sydney, Australia
2004	Athens, Greece
2008	Beijing, China
2012	London, England

❋ THE ORIGINAL FLYING FINN ❋

Juho Pietari ("Hannes") Kolehmainen of Finland, who won three gold medals at the 1912 Olympics in Sweden, was the first of many great Finnish long-distance runners dubbed "The Flying Finns". He won the 5,000 metres in a world record time of 14:36.06 and set a world record time in the 3,000 metres in a heat of the team event. He also won a silver medal with the Finnish team in the cross-country team event. Finland was ruled by Russia at the time, and although Finland sent a team to the Olympics, when a Finnish athlete won gold the Russian flag was raised during the medal ceremony. This led Kolehmainen to say that he almost wished he hadn't won. After the First World War prevented the hosting of the Games of the VI Olympiad, the Belgian city of Antwerp hosted the 1920 Olympics, with Kolehmainen winning the gold medal in the marathon. At the 1912 Games the Finns also won four other track gold medals. Hannes and his brother, Willie, had spent considerable time in the USA training for the Games under the guidance of an American coach, and when they returned home they helped train other Finnish athletes. In 1917 Kolehmainen finished fourth in the Boston Marathon.

❊ OLYMPIC FLAG AT HALF-MAST ❊

On the second day of the 2000 Games the President of the IOC, Juan Antonio Samaranch, had to return home as his wife was severely ill. However, by the time he got there she had already died. Samaranch returned to Sydney four days later and the Olympic flag was flown at half-mast as a mark of respect. Canadia's flag also flew at half-mast in the Olympic Village following the death of their former Prime Minister, Pierre Trudeau.

❊ EIGHT DAYS, SEVEN GOLDS ❊

Over a period of eight days at the 1972 Munich Olympics, Mark Spitz (USA) entered seven swimming events, won all seven and set a new world record in every one. Spitz is the only person to win seven gold medals at a single Olympiad and remains one of only four athletes to win nine career gold medals, having won two golds in Mexico City in 1968.

❊ SECOND WORLD WAR GAMES ❊

The 1940 Olympic Games had been scheduled for Tokyo, Japan, but by mid-1938 Japan was at war with China and withdrew. The IOC then awarded the 1940 Games to Helsinki, Finland, but they also withdrew as hosts after being invaded by the Soviet Union in 1939. The 1944 Olympic Games were scheduled to take place in London but were cancelled as the world was still at war.

❊ A LIVING LEGEND ❊

At the opening ceremony of the 1996 Atlanta Games, one of the oldest living sportsmen was in attendance, 97-year-old gymnast Leon Stukelj from Yugoslavia. In Paris 1924 he won the horizontal bars gold and all-around gold. Four years later, in Amsterdam, he won gold on the rings plus two bronze medals (all-around and team competition). He missed the 1932 Olympics in the USA, like many other athletes who could not afford the cost of crossing the Atlantic. Finally, in the Berlin Games of 1936 he won a silver medal on the rings. At the Atlanta Games he shook hands with President Bill Clinton and was afforded the honour of presenting the medals to winners in the men's team gymnastics competition, much to the delight of both the spectators and the gymnasts. Stukelj died on 12 November 1999, just four days short of his 101st birthday.

❋ TARZAN ENDS JAPANESE RULE ❋

In 1932 Japanese swimmers claimed gold in every men's event except for the 400 metres freestyle, which was won by Larry "Buster" Crabbe from the USA. Crabbe went on to play Tarzan in the 1933 Tarzan TV serial *Tarzan the Fearless*, which was also issued as a full-length film, and starred in more than 100 Hollywood movies. In the women's events, by contrast, the Americans dominated, claiming four of the five gold medals. Helene Madison won gold in the 100 and 400 metres freestyle races and a third gold as a member of the USA relay team.

❋ THE FIRST ALL-ROUND OLYMPIAN ❋

Eric Lemming was born in Goteborg, Sweden, in 1880, and at the age of 19 he set a world record of 49.31 metres in the javelin throw. The following year Lemming travelled to Paris to compete in the Games, but as the javelin was not an Olympic discipline in 1900 the young Swedish athlete participated in six other events. He finished fourth in three events, the high jump, the pole vault and the hammer throw, and eighth in the discus throw. At the 1906 Intercalated Games held in Athens, Lemming competed in nine different events. He won the freestyle javelin throw gold medal, setting a new world record, won bronze medals in the pentathlon, the shot put and the tug of war, and finished a very respectable fourth in the discus and the stone throw. At the London Games of 1908 the javelin throw was finally accepted as an Olympic event while Lemming was still the world record holder in the discipline. Lemming won the freestyle javelin throw in 1908 (after which the event was dropped) and then broke his own world record to claim gold in the regular javelin event with a throw measuring 54.825 metres. He also finished eighth in the hammer throw and participated in the discus throw and the Greek-style discus throw. In 1912, aged 32, Lemming made a final appearance at the 1912 Olympics, which fittingly were held in his home country of Sweden. Lemming did not disappoint the home crowd, winning the gold medal in the javelin with a new world record throw in excess of 60 metres, the first athlete to exceed the mark. The appreciative crowd gave their hero a much deserved standing ovation. Lemming also took fourth place in a one-time event in which the competitors threw the javelin with each hand at the Stockholm Games. During his career, Lemming set 10 javelin world records, including his swan-song, a post-1912 Olympics throw of 62.32 metres. He died in 1930.

❋ THE GAMES OF THE X OLYMPIAD ❋

The 1932 Los Angeles Olympics were officially opened on 30 July 1932 by Charles Curtis, Vice-President of the USA. The opening ceremony took place in the superb Los Angeles Olympic Stadium (later renamed the Los Angeles Memorial Coliseum), where the Olympic oath was given by George Calnan (fencing). Los Angeles had been the only city to offer to host the Games, as the world was still suffering from the effects of the Great Depression, which had begun in 1929. Indeed, because of the high cost of travelling to the USA, the Games managed to attract just over half the number of participants from four years earlier (Amsterdam 1928). However, despite the relatively small number of athletes – 1,332 (1,206 men and 126 women) – the level of competition was extremely high, with no fewer than 18 world records either broken or equalled at the Games (16 of them in men's track and field). The American public warmly welcomed the Olympics to their country with record crowds in attendance, including the 100,000 spectators who attended the opening ceremony. Among the firsts witnessed at the 1932 Games were electronic timing to 1/100th of a second, the use of the photo-finish camera, the three-tier victory podium, and the playing of national anthems and the raising of national flags at the medal ceremonies. The star of the Games was 21-year-old American Mildred Didrikson, who qualified for all five women's track and field events. However, Babe, as she was affectionately nicknamed, was allowed to compete in only three of the events: she won the javelin throw and set world records in the high jump and the 80 metres hurdles to claim three gold medals. A total of 37 nations sent their athletes to participate in 117 events across 14 sports. The closing ceremony took place on 14 August 1920.

Los Angeles 1932 – Final Medals Table (Top Ten)

Pos.	Nation	Gold	Silver	Bronze	Total
1	USA	41	32	30	103
2	Italy	12	12	12	36
3	France	10	5	4	19
4	Sweden	9	5	9	23
5	Japan	7	7	4	18
6	Hungary	6	4	5	15
7	Finland	5	8	12	25
8	Great Britain	4	7	5	16
9	Germany	3	12	5	20
10	Australia	3	1	1	5

❋ 16-YEAR-OLD GOLD MEDAL ❋

Ulrike Meyfarth of West Germany won the gold medal in the high jump at the 1972 Olympics. She beat her personal best by 7cm (first by 5cm and then by another 2cm) to equal the world record (1.92m) and become the youngest person of either sex to win an athletics gold medal in an individual event at an Olympiad. After the 1972 Games her career went on a bit of a rollercoaster. She failed to qualify for the high jump final at the 1976 Olympics in Montreal, could not compete when West Germany boycotted the 1980 Games in Moscow, but claimed her second gold medal in the high jump in Los Angeles in 1984, 12 years after her first. This time she became the oldest female to win the Olympic high jump title.

❋ DUTCH PUBLIC SPONSOR OLYMPIAD ❋

In May 1925, the Dutch Olympic Committee published an appeal in which they asked the general public for help with raising funds to host the 1928 Olympics in Amsterdam. Within two weeks the generous Dutch public donated more than 1.5 million guilders.

❋ FOUR-MINUTE MILER IN THE POOL ❋

At the 1980 Moscow Olympics, Vladimir Salinkov (USSR) won three swimming gold medals (400m freestyle, 1500m freestyle and 4x200m freestyle relay). In the final of the 1500 metres freestyle he won the gold medal in a time of 14:58.27, the first swimmer in history to break the magic 15-minute barrier in the event (considered to be the equivalent of breaking the four-minute barrier for the mile on the track). Salinkov missed the 1984 Olympics in Los Angeles on account of the USSR's boycott of the Games, but four years later he again won gold in the 1500 metres freestyle in Seoul 1988.

❋ OUT OF THE BLACK INTO THE RED ❋

The official budget of the organizing committee for the 1908 London Games was £15,000. More than £5,000 of the budget was put aside for "entertainment expenses", while most of the revenue for the Games did not come from ticket sales (which accounted for 28 per cent of revenue) but from donations. With receipts for the Games totalling £21,377, the organizers claimed a profit. However, they failed to include the construction of the White City Stadium, which cost the British tax-payer £60,000.

❋ OLYMPIC TALK (9) ❋

"I can only say that working with Big John was one of the highlights of my life. He was a Star (with a capital 'S') and he gave off a special light and some of that light got into me. Knowing and being with Johnny Weissmuller during my formative years had a lasting influence on my life."

*Actor **Johnny Sheffield**, who played "Boy" in the Tarzan movies alongside Johnny Weismuller*

❋ A PODIUM OF ONE ❋

During the final of the 400 metres at the 1908 Games a major incident occurred that would later result in a change of the rules at future Olympics. Wyndham Halswelle of Great Britain reached the final after setting the fastest qualifying time, an Olympic record of 48.4 seconds. In the final, Halswelle was up against three other runners, John C. Carpenter, William Robbins and John Taylor, all American. As the four athletes came into the final stretch of the race Robbins was leading, followed by Carpenter, with Halswelle third. Carpenter and Halswelle then both swung out to pass Robbins when a race official, Roscoe Badger, shouted "Foul!" Carpenter crossed the line in first place followed home by Robbins, with Halswelle third. However, the British race officials accused Carpenter of blocking Halswelle and voided the race. Although photographic evidence showed that Carpenter did block Halswelle, under US athletics rules blocking in a race was permitted. However, the 1908 Olympic 400 metres final was being run under the much stricter British rules. The officials ordered a re-run of the race, this time in lanes, and without Carpenter, whom they disqualified. When the remaining two Americans decided not to race, out of loyalty to their team-mate, Halswelle ran the race alone and won the gold medal. It remains the only occasion in Olympic history where the final was a walk-over and as a direct result of the controversy surrounding the race, from the 1912 Games onwards all 400m races were run in lanes.

❋ EAST GERMANY'S GOLDEN GIRL ❋

Kristin Otto of East Germany was the dominant force in the pool in Seoul, winning six gold medals (50m freestyle, 100m butterfly, 100m freestyle, 100m backstroke, 4x100m freestyle and 4x100m medley relay). She was named the Female World Swimmer of the Year in 1984, 1986 and 1988 by *Swimming World* magazine.

Lane No./Athlete	Country	Olympic Medals
1 Irena Szewinska	Poland	Gold – Mexico City 1968, Silver – Tokyo 1964
2 Fanny Blankers-Koen	Netherlands	Gold – London 1948
3 Florence Griffith-Joyner	USA	Gold – Seoul 1988, Silver – Los Angeles 1984
4 Renate Stecher	E. Germany	Gold – Munich 1972, Bronze – Montreal 1976
5 Valerie Brisco-Hooks	USA	Gold – Los Angeles 1984
6 Bärbel Wöckel	E. Germany	2 Gold – Montreal 1976 & Moscow 1980
7 Veronica Campbell	Jamaica	Gold – Athens 2004
8 Gwen Torrance	USA	Gold – Barcelona 1992

✳ JOHNNY WEISSMULLER (1904–84) ✳

Johnny Weissmuller was born in Freidorf, Austria-Hungary (now Romania) on 2 June 1904. When he was seven months old, his family emigrated to the USA. Following a short stay with relatives in Chicago the Weissmullers moved to the coal mining town of Windber, Pennsylvania, before moving back to Chicago to live. As a boy Johnny learned how to swim at the beaches of Lake Michigan, and aged 12 he won a place on the YMCA swim team. At the age of 16 he commenced training at Illinois Athletic Club, Chicago, where under coach "Big Bill" Bachrach's tutelage Weissmuller developed his revolutionary high-riding front crawl. On 6 August 1921 he made his amateur debut, winning his first AAU race in the 50-yard freestyle. However, to earn a spot on the USA Olympic team he had to have an American passport, and so he gave his birthplace as Windber and his birth date as that of his younger brother, Peter Weissmuller, who was born a year after the family arrived in the USA. At that point Johnny became Peter John Weissmuller, born in Pennsylvania in 1905, and Peter became John Peter Weissmuller, born in Austria-Hungary in 1904. Up until his death in 1966 Peter continued to maintain that he was the older brother, protecting Johnny's American identity.

On 9 July 1922, Weissmuller broke Duke Kahanamoku's world record for the 100 metres freestyle, swimming it in a time of 58.6 seconds. At the 1924 Olympics in Paris, Johnny won three gold medals – the 100 metres freestyle, the 400 metres freestyle and the 4x200m freestyle relay – plus a bronze medal in the men's water polo. Four years later, at the Amsterdam Olympics, Johnny retained his 100 metres freestyle crown and claimed a second successive 4x200m freestyle gold. In addition to his six Olympic medals he won 52 US National Championships and set 67 world records, and he retired from his amateur swimming career undefeated. After his swimming career, he signed a contract with BVD in 1929 to be a model and representative, and that same year he made his first film, appearing as an Adonis, wearing only a figleaf, in *Glorifying the American Girl*. His Hollywood career blossomed when he signed a seven-year contract with MGM to play Tarzan in a series of films beginning with *Tarzan the Ape Man* (1932). Johnny went on to have a long and successful career on the silver screen before finally retiring in 1965. He died on 20 January 1984.

Did You Know That?
Johnny Weissmuller's image appeared on the cover of the Beatles' album *Sgt Pepper's Lonely Hearts Club Band*.

❋ ARGENTINA HALT DOMINANT USA ❋

In the men's basketball tournament at the 2004 Games in Athens, Argentina prevented the USA from winning their fourth consecutive gold medal in the competition by defeating them 89–81 in the semi-finals. Argentina went on to beat Italy 84–69 in the final to claim the gold medal, while the USA had to settle for the bronze. In the women's tournament, the USA won their third consecutive Olympic title while Australia claimed the silver and Russia the bronze.

❋ PROFESSIONALS PLAY AT AN OLYMPIAD ❋

For the first time in Olympic history professional footballers were permitted to compete in the football tournament when the Games were held in Los Angeles in 1984. The only condition was that they must not have taken part in a FIFA World Cup. France beat Brazil 2–0 in the final in front of 101,799 spectators at the Rose Bowl, Pasadena. Yugoslavia beat Italy 2–1 in the bronze medal match.

❋ A CASE OF TWO GERMANYS ❋

At the 1952 Olympic Games held in Helsinki, the two Germanys were invited back after a 16-year absence since the "Hitler Olympics" of 1936. West Germany entered under the aegis of a new National Olympic Committee (NOC), the Federal Republic of Germany (FRG). East Germany also established a new NOC after the Second World War, the German Democratic Republic (GDR), but did not send any athletes to the 1952 Games.

❋ VIVE LA FRANCE ❋

Marie-Jose Perec of France won the 200 metres at the Atlanta Games and then broke the 400m Olympic record on her way to a double gold. She also won the 400m title in Barcelona 1992, and during her career she collected two European Championships gold medals and one bronze, plus two gold medals in the World Championships. She remains the most successful French female athlete of all time and the first female athlete to successfully defend the Olympic 400m title. Prior to the Sydney Olympics in 2000, Perec left the Olympic Village in a cloud of controversy and did not compete in the 400 metres against the home favourite, Cathy Freeman, who went on to take the 400m gold medal. Perec had been harassed by the Australian press from the moment she arrived in Sydney.

❋ THE GAMES OF THE XI OLYMPIAD ❋

The 1936 Olympic Games were held in Berlin, Germany. On 1 August 1936, the opening ceremony was held in the purpose-built Olympic Stadium and was officially opened by the German Chancellor, Adolf Hitler. The Nazi propaganda machine attempted to showcase the Games to the world as Hitler's vision of a new Germany, but his plan to prove his theories of Aryan racial superiority backfired on him as the hosts managed to win only a total of five gold medals in track and field events – only one more than the black US athlete Jesse Owens achieved on his own. Owens was the major star of the Games, winning gold medals in the 100m, the 200m, the 4x100m relay and the long jump. German weightlifter Rudolf Ismayr gave the athletes' Olympic oath, and the Olympic flame was lit by the athlete Fritz Schilgen. Only one other city bid to host the 1936 Games, Barcelona, but Berlin's bid was preferred by the IOC in April 1931. It is worth noting that the IOC granted Germany the right to host the Games of the XI Olympiad before the Nazi Party came to power. A total of 49 nations sent 3,963 athletes (3,632 men, 331 women) to participate in 129 events across 19 sports at the Games. The closing ceremony took place on 16 August 1936.

Berlin 1936 – Final Medals Table (Top 10)

Pos.	Nation	Gold	Silver	Bronze	Total
1	Germany	33	26	30	89
2	USA	24	20	12	56
3	Hungary	10	1	5	16
4	Italy	8	9	5	22
5	Finland	7	6	6	19
	France	7	6	6	19
7	Sweden	6	5	9	20
8	Japan	6	4	8	18
9	Netherlands	6	4	7	17
10	Great Britain	4	7	3	14

❋ BITTEN BUT NOT BEATEN ❋

The most controversial gold medal at the 1924 Paris Games was unquestionably that of Harry Mallin in the middleweight division of boxing. Frenchman Roger Brousse was initially declared the winner following his bout with Mallin, but a Swedish official complained that the Briton had been bitten by his opponent during the fight, and Brousse was disqualified.

✳ KEEP YOUR MEDALS, WE DON'T WANT 'EM ✳

The USA's men's basketball team first lost a game in Olympic competition at Munich in 1972. They went into the 1972 final against the USSR with an unblemished 62–0 record dating back to 1936. With just three seconds of the game left on the clock, the USSR led 49–48 before committing a hard foul on Doug Collins. Collins made two free throws to put the USA 50–49 in front. The Brazilian referee, Renaldo Righetto, blew his whistle to restart play with a single second of the game remaining. However, the coach of the USSR team, Vladimir Kondrashkin, called for a time-out in between Collins's free throws – although the rules of the game clearly state that a coach cannot call a time-out during free throws. The USA intercepted the inbound pass and began to celebrate victory on the court. However, the General Secretary of FIBA, R. William Jones of Great Britain, permitted the time-out and ordered that three seconds be placed on the game clock. When the Russians inbounded the ball, Alexander Belov scored a lay-up to claim a dramatic 51–50 victory. The USA team refused to accept the silver medal during the medal ceremony and lodged an appeal. However, this was rejected in a 3–2 vote by the five-judge appeal panel made up of judges from Cuba (against), Hungary (against), Italy (for), Poland (against) and Puerto Rico (for). The 1972 Olympic basketball final is considered to be the most controversial game in international basketball history.

✳ MODERN PENTATHLON FIRST ✳

Women took part in the modern pentathlon for the first time in Olympic history at the 2000 Games, and it was joy for Great Britain as Stephanie Cook won the gold medal. Emily de Riel from the USA took the silver, and Britain's Kate Allenby the bronze. Cook was a rower at Cambridge and took up the modern pentathlon only while completing her clinical medicine course at Oxford.

✳ NINE OLYMPIADS ✳

Austrian sailor Hubert Raudaschl became the first person ever to compete in nine Olympiads when he attended the Atlanta Games in 1996. His consecutive Games appearances began in Tokyo 1964, and he narrowly missed out on 10 successive Olympiads as he was a reserve for Rome 1960. Raudaschl won two silver medals, one in the Finn class in Mexico City 1968 and the other in Moscow 1980 in the Star class.

✳ TOO DRUNK TO COMPETE ✳

Naim Suleymanoglu was born in Ptichar, Bulgaria, but represented Turkey in weightlifting. In 1986, during a trip to the Weightlifting World Cup finals in Melbourne, Australia, he defected and ended up in Turkey, where he successfully applied for citizenship. He won three Olympic gold medals (1988 Seoul, 1992 Barcelona and 1996 Atlanta) in the featherweight division (56–60kg), seven World Championships and six European Championships. He also broke world records a staggering 46 times. Standing just 4 foot 11 inches (150 cm) tall, he was nicknamed "the Pocket Hercules". At the 2000 Olympics in Sydney he missed out on his fourth consecutive gold medal when he had three unsuccessful attempts to lift 145 kilos (which was higher than the Olympic record). In 2001 he was awarded the Olympic Order.

✳ UNUSUAL SPORTS OF 1900 ✳

Some quite unusual sporting events were contested for the first and only time in Paris 1900. These included the equestrian high and long jumps, live pigeon shooting, a swimming obstacle race and underwater swimming. The obstacle race required both swimming underneath and climbing over rows of boats. In the underwater swimming event Charles de Venville of France won gold after staying submerged for over one minute. Meanwhile the Belgian athlete, Leon Lunden, shot 21 birds on his way to the live pigeon shooting gold medal.

✳ ROMANS END PAGAN GAMES ✳

After Greece became part of the Roman Empire in 146 BC, the Olympic Games, which had begun in 776 BC, continued for several centuries. After the Christianization of Rome, however, the Games came to be viewed as a pagan festival and in contravention of Christian values. In AD 393, the Emperor Theodosius I banned the Olympics, bringing an end to a tradition that had lasted more than 1,000 years.

✳ TARZAN THE MARATHON MAN ✳

Johnny Weissmuller, who starred in the 1924 and 1928 Olympiads, winning five gold medals, and who played Tarzan in a number of Hollywood movies, also won the Chicago marathon twice.

❋ WAR HERO AND GREAT OLYMPIAN ❋

In 1908 George Yvan ("Geo") Andre of France made his Olympic debut in the high jump at the age of 18. Prior to arriving in England for the Games his best ever jump was 1.79 metres, but in the White City Stadium he cleared 1.88 metres and won the silver medal. Four years later in Stockholm, Andre entered the 110 metres hurdles, the decathlon, the high jump, the pentathlon, the standing high jump and the standing long jump. During the First World War he fought as a soldier, was seriously injured and then captured and imprisoned by the Germans. After making numerous attempts to escape he finally succeeded and rejoined the French forces as a fighter pilot and won a military medal. At the Games held in Antwerp, Belgium, in 1920 he won a bronze medal in the 4x400m relay. When the Olympics returned to Paris in 1924, the city of his birth, he was selected to take the Olympic oath on behalf of all the athletes. In Paris, at 34 years of age and participating in his fourth Olympics, he finished fourth in the 400 metres hurdles for the second successive Games. In total he competed in 13 different disciplines spanning four Olympiads.

❋ OLYMPIC TALK (10) ❋

"The Olympics are always a special competition. It is very difficult to predict what will happen."
Sergei Bubka, Ukrainian pole vaulter, 1988 Games

❋ AND LET THE GAMES BEGIN ❋

At the inaugural meeting of the International Olympic Committee held in the Sorbonne, Paris, in 1894, Baron Pierre de Coubertin proposed that the Olympic Games should be revived and that the first modern Games should be held in Paris in 1900 to coincide with the Universal Exhibition or World's Fair planned for the city in 1900. The delegates from the 10 other countries represented at the Congress did not want to wait six years to revive the Games, and some of them proposed London as a venue for the first modern Games, to be held in 1896. However, de Coubertin was against London staging the event and so he proposed Athens. De Coubertin's fellow delegates unanimously agreed with his nomination, as Athens was the original home of the Olympics. The Greek delegate at the Congress, Demetrius Vikelas, was elected as the first President of the newly established International Olympic Committee (IOC).

✳ LIGHTBODY CLEANS UP ✳

Jim Lightbody of the USA won three gold medals at the 1904 Olympics: in the 2,500m steeplechase, the 800 metres and, finally, the 1500 metres, in which he set a new world record on his way to gold. On the same day that he broke the 1500m world record, Lightbody won a silver medal in the four-mile team event with his Chicago Athletic Association team-mates. At the Intercalated Olympics held in Athens in 1906, he successfully defended his 1500m title and took silver in the 800m to bring to his total to six Olympic medals. However, during the early part of the twentieth century the IOC downgraded the 1906 Games, resulting in the non-recognition by the IOC of the two medals he won in Athens.

✳ RAINCOAT FOR A GOLD MEDAL ✳

The final of the women's 4x400 metres relay at the 1948 London Olympics was held on the final day of the track and field competitions. The Dutch team had qualified for the final, but with the race drawing near it was discovered that their sprint star, Fanny Blankers-Koen, who had already won three gold medals at the Games (100m, 200m & 80m hurdles), was missing. She had gone shopping for a raincoat, but returned in time to anchor the Dutch team to victory over the Australians.

Did You Know That?
On 7 August 1955, Fanny Blankers-Koen won her last event, the national title in the shot put, her 58th Dutch title.

✳ WATER BABIES ✳

Hungary's Deszo Gyarmati is the greatest water polo player in the history of the sport. Gyarmati won five Olympic medals at five successive Olympiads (gold in 1952, 1956 & 1964; silver in 1948; bronze in 1960) and captained Hungary to victory in the 1954 and 1962 European Water Polo Championships. After his playing career ended he coached the Hungarian national water polo team that won gold at the 1976 Olympics in Montreal. Gyarmati married Eva Szekely, winner of the 200m breaststroke gold medal at the 1952 Olympics, and their daughter Andrea won a silver medal at the 1972 Olympics in Munich, Germany in the 100 metres backstroke. Andrea married Mihaly Hesz, Hungary's 1968 Olympic canoeing champion.

❋ OLYMPISM ❋

Olympism is a state of mind based on equality of sports that are international and democratic. Furthermore, it is a philosophy of life, whereby athletes utilize the qualities of their body, their determination and their mind to "go faster, further and higher".

❋ NO WORLD RECORDS ❋

No world records were set at the Games of 1896, mainly owing to the fact that few of the world's top athletes had travelled to Greece to take part. Thomas Burke of the USA won both the 100 metres and the 400 metres in times of 12.0 seconds and 54.2 seconds.

❋ BOYCOTT BENEFACTORS ❋

At the Moscow Games of 1980 the Italians and French benefited from the US-led boycott: the Italians won eight gold medals, four times as many as in Montreal, where they won two, while the French claimed six golds in Moscow, compared with their two in Montreal. The Moscow Olympics was also the most successful Olympiad since Melbourne 1956 for a number of other nations, including Great Britain and Ireland, while Bulgaria and Spain won their first ever medals in men's track events. In total, athletes from 25 different countries won gold, and athletes from 36 different countries took home a medal.

❋ SHOW ME THE MONEY ❋

At Amsterdam in 1928 spectators could purchase souvenirs depicting the five Olympic rings for the first time. The commercialization of the Games had begun.

❋ "BARCELONA" ❋

The main musical theme of the 1992 Olympic Games was a song entitled "Barcelona", written in 1987 by Freddie Mercury, the lead singer of Queen. Freddie was to have sung the song as a duet with Montserrat Caballe, the Spanish operatic soprano, during the opening ceremony. However, because of Mercury's untimely death on 24 November 1991, the song was used instead to accompany a film celebrating the city that was shown at the beginning of the opening ceremony.

✳ THE GAMES OF THE XIV OLYMPIAD ✳

The 1948 Olympic Games were held in London, the second time the British capital played host to an Olympiad. Because of the Second World War the Games of the XII and XIII Olympiads had been cancelled. The opening ceremony took place in Wembley Stadium on 29 July 1948 and the Games were officially opened by HRH King George VI. In the women's foil fencing Hungary's Ilona Elek retained her crown, while Czech canoeist Jan Brzak won a second successive gold medal in the canoeing Canadian pairs 1,000 metres. US athlete Bob Mathias, aged only 17, caused a sensation at the Games by winning gold in the decathlon just two months after graduating from high school and only four months after taking up the sport. To this day he remains the youngest Olympian in history to win a men's event in athletics. Fanny Blankers-Koen, a 30-year-old mother of two from the Netherlands, went into the Games as the world record holder in six events (80m hurdles, 100m, 200m, 4x100m relay, high jump and long jump) but she was only permitted to compete in four events under Olympic rules at the time. She dropped the high jump and the long jump and won a gold medal in each of the other four. John Mark (athletics) lit the Olympic flame, and his team-mate Donald Finlay (athletics) gave the Olympic oath. A total of 59 nations sent 4,104 athletes (3,714 men, 390 women) to participate in 136 events across 17 sports at the Games. The closing ceremony took place on 14 August 1948.

London 1948 – Final Medals Table (Top 10)

Pos.	Nation	Gold	Silver	Bronze	Total
1	USA	38	27	19	84
2	Sweden	16	11	17	44
3	France	10	6	13	29
4	Hungary	10	5	12	27
5	Italy	8	11	8	27
6	Finland	8	7	5	20
7	Turkey	6	4	2	12
8	Czechoslovakia	6	2	3	11
9	Switzerland	5	10	5	20
10	Denmark	5	7	8	20

✳ SEVEN-GAMES WOMAN ✳

Kerstin Palm, a Swedish fencer, became the first woman to take part in seven Olympics when she represented her country at the 1988 Games.

❈ THE FRIENDSHIP GAMES ❈

The Soviet-led boycott of the 1984 Games resulted in the athletes of 14 nations staying at home. At the Montreal Olympics, however, these 14 had won a staggering 51 per cent of the medals (58 per cent of the gold medals). The boycotting nations now organized the "Friendship Games" (Druzhba-84), which were held in nine different countries between July and September 1984 and included 24 Olympic sports in the programme. In 28 of the 41 track events the winning time set by an athlete at the Friendship Games was lower than that of the 1984 Olympic gold medallist. Evelyn Ashford of the USA won the women's 100m gold medal in Los Angeles in a time of 10.97 seconds, whereas Marlies Gohr of East Germany won the Friendship Games final in 10.95 seconds. While 21 world records were set in Los Angeles, over twice as many were set at Druzhba-84 (48, of which 22 were set by athletes from the USSR).

❈ ON YOUR BLOCKS ❈

In 1948 starting blocks were introduced for the first time and used in races from 100 metres to 400 metres.

❈ THE GENERAL'S DIARY ❈

Among the competitors at Stockholm 1912 was George S. Patton, the future Second World War general. Patton participated in the first modern pentathlon competition, finishing fifth behind four Swedes.

❈ FLYING IN THIN AIR ❈

Bob Beamon of the USA shattered the world record in the long jump at the 1968 Mexico City Olympics with an enormous first leap of 8.90 metres (29 feet, 2½ inches), beating the existing world record mark by almost two feet. Whereas the altitude (7,349 feet above sea level) affected a number of the athletes, it appeared to help Beamon glide over the sand pit beneath him. Beamon's jump was so long that the judges had to use a metal tape measure after the optical measuring device slid off its rail.

❈ NO MORE CINDERS ❈

Tokyo 1964 was the last time a cinder running track was used in the athletics events at an Olympiad.

❋ OLYMPIC TALK (11) ❋

"When we stage the Olympics it will inspire kids all over the country. A kid in Scotland or Ireland will be encouraged to take up sport."
Daley Thompson, *double Olympic decathlon gold medal winner*

❋ SWIMMER STRIPPED OF GOLD ❋

Rick DeMont of the USA won the 400m freestyle gold medal in the 1972 Olympics. However, the 16-year-old had his gold medal stripped away from him when traces of the banned substance ephedrine were found in a post-race urine test. DeMont had only been taking drugs to control his asthma and had actually disclosed the medication he was taking on his medical statement prior to the Games. The gold medal was awarded to Brad Cooper of Australia. In December 2001, the USOC finally admitted that it had erred in its handling of DeMont's medical information in Munich, but the IOC has yet to give him his medal back.

❋ GOLD FOR LENNOX LEWIS ❋

Lennox Lewis, fighting for Canada, won the super-heavyweight (91 kg and over) gold medal at the 1988 Olympics, beating Riddick Bowe in the final. Both fighters went on to win world heavyweight boxing championships during their careers.

❋ THE SPARROW FROM MINSK ❋

Russian gymnast Olga Korbut won six Olympic medals, four gold and two silver. She burst on to the world scene at the 1972 Olympics in Munich, where her warm smile and captivating performances melted the hearts of the audience at a time when the Cold War was still being played out. In Munich "The Sparrow from Minsk" won gold in the team competition, gold in the balance beam and gold in the floor exercise. At the Games she became the first gymnast ever to do a backward somersault on the balance beam (known as the "Korbut Flip") and was also the first gymnast to do a standing backward somersault on the uneven bars. She also won a silver medal in the uneven bars in Munich. Four years later in Montreal, where Romania's Nadia Comaneci was the star of the Games, winning three gold medals, Olga claimed her fourth gold medal (team competition) plus a silver medal on the balance beam.

※ TRYING TO MAKE A SPLASH ※

Held at the port of Kiel, water skiing was one of the demonstration sports at the 1972 Olympic Games. A total of 35 competitors representing 20 nations took to the water, with the unofficial gold medals awarded across three disciplines – slalom, figure skating and jumping – for both men and women.

※ FIRST AFRICAN OLYMPIANS ※

Among the marathon runners at the 1904 St Louis Games were Len Tau and Jan Mashiani, a pair of Tswana tribesmen in St Louis as part of the Boer War Exhibition at the World's Fair, and they became the first Africans to compete in the Olympics. Tau finished ninth and Mashiani finished twelfth, but had Tau not been chased nearly a mile off course by a large, aggressive dog he might have won the race.

※ ASTERIX AT THE OLYMPICS ※

The live action movie *Asterix and Obelix at the Olympic Games* was released in the run-up to the 2008 Olympic Games in Beijing. In this Olympic story the Gauls, on hearing that the Romans are planning to send legionary Gluteus Maximus to represent Rome at the Olympiad in Greece, decide to send their own champions Asterix and Obelix. Unfortunately for them, the Greek officials ban the magic potion as it is an artificial stimulant, and so Asterix and Obelix must compete as mere mortals. However, Asterix manages to persuade the Romans to drink the potion, which sees them kicked out of the Games, leaving Asterix the winner of the "Golden Palm". The famous French actor, Gérard Depardieu, returns for the third time as Obelix.

Did You Know That?
When Paris was bidding to host the 1992 Olympics, their bid committee published a poster depicting Asterix holding a torch over the Eiffel Tower, while a brief "Asterix at the Olympics" story was also written to promote the bid. The IOC chose Barcelona as the host city.

※ LEAST POPULATED MEDAL WINNERS ※

In 1976 Bermuda, with a mere 53,500 inhabitants, became the least populated country to win a medal at an Olympiad when boxer Clarence Hill won the bronze medal in the heavyweight division at the Montreal Games.

❉ MORE THAN AN ATHLETICS STADIUM ❉

The following stadia that have played host to an Olympic Games
have also hosted other major sporting events:

Athens – Olympiako Stadio

1983 European Cup Final, 1994 and 2007 UEFA Champions
League Finals, 1997 World Championships in Athletics,
2007WRC Acropolis Rally SuperSpecial Stage 2005 and 2006
2006 IAAF World Cup

Berlin – Olympiastadion

2006 FIFA World Cup Final

Helsinki – Olympiastadion

1983 and 2005 IAAF World Championships

London – Wembley Stadium (original)

1966 FIFA World Cup Final, 1996 UEFA European Championship
Final, five UEFA European Cup Finals 1963–92

London – White City Stadium

1934 Empire Games

Los Angeles – Memorial Coliseum

Super Bowl I (1967), Super Bowl VII (1973), 1959 World Series

Melbourne – Melbourne Cricket Ground

1992 Cricket World Cup Final, 2006 Commonwealth Games,
annual Australian Football League Grand Final

Munich – Olympiastadion

1974 FIFA World Cup Final, 1979 European Cup Final, 1988
UEFA European Championship Final, 1993 and 1997 UEFA
Champions League Finals

Paris – Stade Olympique de Colombes

1938 FIFA World Cup Final

Rome – Stadio Olimpico

1977 and 1984 European Cup Finals, 1987 IAAF World
Championships, 1990 FIFA World Cup Final, 1996 UEFA
Champions League Final

Sydney – Stadium Australia (now Telstra Stadium)

2003 Rugby World Cup Final, annual National Rugby League
Grand Final

Tokyo – National Olympic Stadium

1991 IAAF World Championships

❉ A FALL FROM GRACE ❉

The USA men's gymnastics team won gold at the 1984 Los Angeles
Olympics. Four years later in Seoul they finished in 11th place.

❋ FANTASY MEN'S 400M OLYMPIC FINAL ❋

Lane No./Athlete		*Country*	*Olympic Medals*
1	Alberto Juantorena	Cuba	Gold – Montreal 1976
2	Eric Liddell	GB	Gold – Paris 1924
3	Michael Johnson	USA	2 Gold – Atlanta 1996 & Sydney 2000
4	George Rhoden	Jamaica	Gold – Helsinki 1952
5	Viktor Markin	USSR	Gold – Moscow 1980
6	Jeremy Warner	USA	Gold – Athens 2004
7	Quincy Watts	USA	Gold – Barcelona 1992
8	Steve Lewis	USA	Gold – Seoul 1988, Silver – Barcelona 1992

❀ THE GAMES OF THE XV OLYMPIAD ❀

The 1952 Helsinki Olympics were officially opened by President Juho Kusti Paasikivi on 19 July 1952 at the Helsinki Olympic Stadium. However, prior to President Paasikivi's official opening speech the spectators watched as Paavo Nurmi, Finland's nine times Olympic champion (1920, 1924 & 1928), entered the stadium with the Olympic flame. The 55-year-old Nurmi lit a cauldron on the ground, and young football players then carried the torch up to the top of the stadium tower, where another former Finnish Olympic champion, Hannes Kolehmainen (four athletics gold medals, 1912 & 1920), lit the Olympic cauldron. Heikki Savolainen (gymnastics) gave the Olympic oath. Both Nurmi and Kölehmainen, middle- and long-distance running champions, would have been impressed with the exploits of Emil Zatopek of Czechoslovakia at the Helsinki Games. Zatopek became the only person in Olympic history to win the 5,000 metres, the 10,000 metres and the marathon at the same Games. The 1952 Helsinki Olympics witnessed the first ever participation at an Olympiad by the Soviet Union (Russia competed in the 1912 Games) although they insisted that their athletes live in a separate "Olympic Village". Indeed, the Soviet women's gymnastics team impressed everyone with their athleticism by winning the team competition very comfortably, thereby beginning a winning streak that would last for almost 10 Olympiads until the Soviet Union broke up into separate republics. Israel also made their inaugural appearance at the 1952 Olympic Games in Helsinki, while women were permitted to compete against men in the Olympic equestrian dressage event for the first time. A total of 69 nations sent 4,955 athletes (4,436 men, 519 women) to participate in 149 events across 17 sports. The closing ceremony took place on 3 August 1952.

Helsinki 1952 – Final Medals Table (Top 10)

Pos.	Nation	Gold	Silver	Bronze	Total
1	USA	40	19	17	76
2	USSR	22	30	19	71
3	Hungary	16	10	16	42
4	Sweden	12	13	10	35
5	Italy	8	9	4	21
6	Czechoslovakia	7	3	3	13
7	France	6	6	6	18
8	Finland	6	3	13	22
9	Australia	6	2	3	11
10	Norway	3	2	0	5

❆ OLYMPIC TORCH REIGNITED ❆

At the Los Angeles Memorial Coliseum the Olympic cauldron was built specially for the 1932 Olympic Games (it was used again in 1984 when the Games returned to the city). In fact the cauldron is still lit on a regular basis. It is seen most often during the fourth quarter of USC (University of Southern California) American football games, and also when an Olympiad is on, regardless of location. In addition, the cauldron is lit to mark other special occasions: in 2004, after former US President Ronald Reagan died, it was ignited for a week as a mark of respect; in April 2005, following the death of Pope John Paul II – who had celebrated a mass at the stadium on his 1987 visit – the cauldron was ignited once more; and it also had been lit for around 10 days following the 11 September terror attacks on the USA in 2001.

❆ CHARIOTS OF FIRE ❆

At the 1924 Paris Olympics, two British runners, Harold Abrahams and Eric Liddell, won gold medals in the 100 metres and the 400 metres respectively. Their achievements were documented in the 1981 Hugh Hudson Academy Award-winning film *Chariots of Fire*. In one important detail, however, the film is not historically accurate. Liddell, a devout Christian, knew many months in advance that the preliminary heats for the 100 metres (his favoured event) would take place on a Sunday, and so, contrary to the story in the film, he had plenty of time to alter his training and prepare for the 400 metres.

❆ TWENTIETH-CENTURY MASTER OF DISASTER ❆

During the 1960 Rome Games, 18-year-old Cassius Marcellus Clay, later known as Muhammad Ali, won a gold medal in boxing's light-heavyweight division, defeating his Polish opponent, Zbigniew Pietryskowsky, in the final. Ali would go on to become the undisputed heavyweight boxing champion of the world and one of the greatest sporting icons of the twentieth century.

❆ ABOVE ALL OTHERS ❆

At the London Games of 1908, Ray Ewry from the USA won the standing high jump and the standing long jump for the third consecutive Olympics. Ewry is the only person in Olympic history to win a career total of eight gold medals in individual events.

❉ BABE ZAHARIAS (1911–56) ❉

Mildred Ella "Babe" Didrikson Zaharias was born on 26 June 1911 in Port Arthur, Texas. She was nicknamed "Babe", having hit five home runs in one game of baseball, after the legendary Babe Ruth. In 1930 Babe obtained a job as a secretary with the Employers Casualty Insurance Co., Dallas, Texas, and led her works team to an AAU Basketball Championship in 1931 and also represented her company in the 1932 AAU Championships, entering eight events, winning five outright and tying first for a sixth. Amazingly, she set five world records in a single afternoon at the championships. Babe was a sporting phenomenon and gained world fame in track and field at the 1932 Summer Olympics in Los Angeles: she won the gold medal in the 80 metres hurdles in an Olympic record time of 11.7 seconds; she won the gold medal in the javelin with a throw of 143 feet, 4 inches, another Olympic record; and she tied with Jean Shiley for the 1932 Olympics high jump title with an Olympic record clearance of 5 feet, 5 inches. At the time Miss Shiley was presented the gold medal and Babe was given the silver medal, because the judges penalized Babe for using the "Western roll" (jumping over head first). Babe was subsequently credited with the Olympic first-place tie. She achieved All-American status in basketball, was an excellent tennis player and an accomplished baseball and softball player, and was also an expert diver, roller-skater and bowler.

In 1935 Babe started to play golf, and after being denied amateur status she competed in the 1938 Los Angeles Open, a men's PGA tournament. It would be almost 60 years before another woman entered a men's PGA Tour event. During her career as a golfer, both amateur and pro, Babe had no equal among women. She won every Major professional championship at least once, and in 1947 became the first American to capture the British Women's Amateur Championship and the first player to win both the US Women's Amateur and the British Women's Amateur. She dominated the sport in the 1940s and the early 1950s, winning 17 amateur tournaments in a row, including the British Amateur, the US Amateur and the All-American (a feat unequalled even by Tiger Woods). Babe's greatest year was 1950, when she became the fastest LPGA golfer ever to reach 10 wins, completed the Grand Slam of the three women's Majors of the day, the US Open, the Titleholders Championship and the Western Open, as well as leading the money list. During her 20-year golf career she won 82 tournaments.

Did You Know That?
Babe Zaharias's Olympic medal for the high jump was actually half gold and half silver, the only such medal in Olympic history.

❋ OLYMPIC TALK (12) ❋

"The greatest memory for me of the 1984 Olympics was not the individual honours, but standing on the podium with my team-mates to receive our team gold medal."
***Mitch Gaylord**, American gymnast, 1984 Games*

❋ BOND, JAMES BOND ❋

Toshiyuki "Harold" Sakata was born on 1 July 1920 in Holualoa, Hawaii, of Japanese descent. At the 1948 London Olympics he won a silver medal for the USA in the heavyweight weightlifting division, lifting a total of 410kg. However, Harold is better known for his role as Oddjob, the villain in the James Bond film *Goldfinger*.

❋ SUPER DALEY ❋

Daley Thompson won the first of his two Olympic decathlon gold medals at the Moscow Games. He also won a gold medal at the World Championships and two European Championships and three Commonwealth Games gold medals in the decathlon. Daley's athletic success during the 1980s led to his name being used for three officially licensed home computer games manufactured by Ocean Software: Daley Thompson's Decathlon, Daley Thompson's Supertest and Daley Thompson's Olympic Challenge.

❋ THE GOLDEN GIRLS ❋

Great Britain's Ann Packer won a gold medal in the 800 metres in Tokyo. Packer had gone to the Games with her sights on winning a gold medal in her favoured event, the 400 metres, but in that she could manage only a silver medal, finishing second to Betty Cuthbert of the USA. With her heart set on coming home with a gold medal Packer entered the 800 metres, a distance she had run competitively only five times previously. In her 800m heat she finished fifth and then claimed third place in the semi-final to secure a place in the final with the slowest qualifying time of the eight athletes in the field. In the final Packer started slowly and was trailing in sixth place after 400 metres, moved up to third after 600 and then with an incredible burst of speed she took the lead in the final straight and raced to victory. It would take four decades for another British athlete, Kelly Holmes, to win the women's 800m Olympic gold, in Athens 2004.

❋ THE ENDURANCE OLYMPICS ❋

During the Stockholm Games of 1912, the course for the cycling road race stretched over 199 miles (320km), making it the longest race of any kind in Olympic history. The riders had to start at 2 a.m. In Greco-Roman wrestling, the middleweight silver medal decider between the Estonian (competing for Russia) Martin Klein and Finland's Alfred Asikainen lasted 11 hours and 40 minutes. Klein won, but he was too exhausted to wrestle in the final the following day, so the gold medal went to Sweden's Claes Johanson. Juho Pietari ("Hannes") Kolehmainen of Finland won three gold medals in long-distance running: the 5,000 metres, the 10,000 metres and the individual cross-country. However, the most popular athlete at the Games was undoubtedly Jim Thorpe of the USA. He won the pentathlon and then went on to shatter the world record in the decathlon.

❋ HELSINKI HERO ❋

During the 1948 Olympic Games held in London, Emil Zatopek won the 10,000 metres in commanding style. On lap 10 of 25 inside Wembley Stadium he moved out in front and lapped all but two of his rivals, claiming the gold medal by a full 300 metres. Three days later the Czechoslovakian ran in the final of the 5,000 metres. His efforts in the 10,000 metres appeared to be taking their toll when going into the final lap he trailed the leader, Belgium's Gaston Reiff, by 50 metres. Zatopek then kicked into gear and almost pipped the Belgian on the line but could manage only a silver medal, finishing just 1.5 metres behind Reiff. Four years later in Helsinki, at the Games of the XV Olympiad, Zatopek retained his Olympic 10,000m title and claimed a third Olympic gold medal by winning the 5,000 metres. Zatopek then decided to enter the marathon, although he had never run one before, and won it by 2½ minutes, much to the appreciation of the Finnish spectators, who sang his name. Emil Zatopek is the only runner in Olympic history to win the long-distance treble of 5,000 metres, 10,000 metres and marathon at a single Olympiad. In 1956 at the Melbourne Games, he was due to run in the marathon but suffered a hernia just six weeks before the Games got under way. He ran anyway and finished in sixth place.

Did You Know That?
On the afternoon of Zatopek's 5,000m triumph, his wife Dana won a gold medal in the javelin throw.

❋ PRINCESS ANNE MISSES SEX TEST ❋

Princess Anne was the only female competitor at the 1976 Montreal Olympics who was not required to have a sex test. She was a member of Great Britain's equestrian team.

❋ USA MEN RULE ❋

In the track and field events at the 1976 Games, the USA men obliterated all before them. Of the 24 events contested an American athlete won 15; the team achieved a 1–2–3 in four of them (200m, 110m hurdles, 400m hurdles and the discus throw) and finished first and second in five others (100m, pole vault, long jump, shot put and decathlon). The American women were not as successful, claiming just two medals from the nine events: Mildred McDaniel's gold in the high jump and a team bronze in the 4x100m relay. Only two world records were set in track and field, and McDaniel claimed one of them with a high jump leap of 5 feet, 9¼ inches. Norway's Egil Danielsen set the other in the men's javelin with a throw of 281 feet, 2½ inches.

❋ HITLER WATCHES STUDENTS WIN GOLD ❋

The USA's eight-man rowing team, all members of the University of Washington, won the gold medal in Berlin by coming from behind to defeat the Germans (who came third) and Italians (second) as Hitler looked on.

❋ MARATHON WINNER ALMOST DIES ❋

Thomas J. Hicks, a brass worker from Cambridge, Massachusetts, won the marathon at the St Louis Olympics in a time of 3 hours, 28 minutes and 53 seconds. However, Hicks's win is clouded in controversy as he walked part of the route and was assisted along the way by substances which are now illegal. When Hicks was struggling in the St Louis heat his assistants dosed him with 1/60th of a grain (approximately 1mg) of strychnine sulphate (now banned by the IOC) and a raw egg white. The first dose of strychnine did not revive him for long, however, and he was given a second dose along with some brandy. The drugs proved too much for his body to take and he had to be helped across the finish line before collapsing. Had Hicks not received medical attention after the race ended he might well have died, and the day after he won his gold medal he announced his retirement from the sport.

❊ THE GAMES OF THE XVI OLYMPIAD ❊

The 1956 Melbourne Olympics were officially opened on 22 November 1956 by HRH the Duke of Edinburgh in the Melbourne Cricket Ground. Ron Clarke (athletics) lit the Olympic flame while John Landy (athletics) gave the Olympic oath at the first ever Olympiad to be held in the southern hemisphere. The Melbourne Games witnessed some outstanding sporting achievements: Hungary's Laszlo Papp became the first boxer to win three successive gold medals when he won the light-middleweight event to add to the light-middleweight gold he won at Helsinki in 1952 and the middleweight gold he won at the London Games in 1948. In gymnastics, two athletes dominated the Games: Viktor Chukarin (Ukraine) won five medals, including three gold (parallel bars, team competition and all-around individual), bringing his career total to 11 medals (seven gold); and Hungary's Agnes Keleti won four gold medals (team portable apparatus, uneven bars, balance beam and floor exercise) and two silver to bring her career tally to ten medals (five gold, three silver, two bronze). The equestrian events had to be held in Stockholm, Sweden, in June 1956 as Australian quarantine laws were too severe to allow the entry of foreign horses. This was the first time in Olympic history that an Olympiad was held in two countries. A total of 72 nations sent 3,314 athletes (2,038 men, 376 women) to participate in 145 events across 17 sports. The closing ceremony took place on 8 December 1956.

Melbourne 1956 – Final Medals Table (Top 10)

Pos.	Nation	Gold	Silver	Bronze	Total
1	USSR	37	29	32	98
2	USA	32	25	17	74
3	Australia	13	8	14	35
4	Hungary	9	10	7	26
5	Italy	8	8	9	25
6	Sweden	8	5	6	19
7	United Germany	6	13	7	26
8	Great Britain	6	7	11	24
9	Romania	5	3	5	13
10	Japan	4	10	5	19

❊ OLYMPIAN ROCKET MAN ❊

During the opening ceremony Bill Suitor flew into the Los Angeles Coliseum powered by a Jet Pack (the Bell Aerosystems Rocket Pack).

❋ WOMEN'S RIGHTS ❋

The programme for 1928 Amsterdam Olympics contained athletics events for women for the first time. However, in his greeting message Baron Pierre de Coubertin wrote: "I'm still an opponent of women participating in the Olympic Games. Against my will, this has become permitted in an ever increasing number of events."

❋ THE RED FLYING MACHINE ❋

Valeri Borzov of the USSR was the sprint king of the 1972 Olympic Games, winning both the 100m and 200m gold medals. Amazingly, the top two sprinters in the USA and clear favourites to take the gold and silver medals in the 100 metres final, Eddie Hayes and Rey Robinson, won their opening rounds but missed their next heat when their coach gave them the wrong starting time. Both athletes were eliminated from the competition.

❋ ISRAEL WINS FIRST MEDAL ❋

Almost 20 years after the Munich Massacre, Yael Arad became the first Israeli to win an Olympic medal when she won silver in judo (61kg class) at the 1992 Games. A day later, fellow judoka Oren Smadja became the first Israeli man to win a medal, bronze, in the 71kg class.

❋ THE HITLER OLYMPICS ❋

On the second day of the 1936 Olympic Games in Berlin, Der Fuhrer, Adolf Hitler, shook hands with two of the gold medal winners from the first two days' events, one German and one Finn, and then left the stadium. At the time many sports writers inferred that Hitler left Berlin's Olympic Stadium so as to avoid having to shake hands with Cornelius Johnson, an African-American who had won the high jump gold medal on that day of the Games. However, according to an official spokesman Hitler's early departure had been pre-scheduled. Following this, IOC officials insisted that the German Chancellor should meet and greet each and every medallist or none at all. Hitler elected to miss all further medal presentations.

❋ CAMEROON WIN SHOOTOUT GOLD ❋

In the Olympic football final of 2000, Cameroon beat Spain 5–3 in a penalty shootout to win the gold medal after the game ended 2–2.

❋ OLYMPIC TALK (13) ❋

"All I've done is run fast. I don't see why people should make much fuss about that."
*Dutch athlete, **Fanny Blankers-Koen**, the biggest star of the 1948 Olympic Games*

❋ TESTING THE WINNERS ❋

During the Mexico City Olympics, in addition to the regular random drugs test, every gold medal winner was required to undergo a drug test. Now all the medal winners are routinely tested.

❋ OLYMPIAN SUPERMAN ❋

Jesse Owens's greatest achievement came in a span of 45 minutes on 25 May 1935 at a track and field meeting in Ann Arbor, Michigan, USA. During the 1935 National Collegiate Athletic Association (NCAA) Championships, Owens set three world records and tied a fourth. He set a new world record in the long jump with a distance of 26 feet 8¼ inches, or 8.13m (a mark that would stand for 25 years); he set a new world record in the 220 yards (200m) with a time of 20.3 seconds; he set a new world record in the 220 yards (200m) low hurdles in a time of 22.6 seconds (the first person to break 23 seconds); and he tied the world record for the 100 yards (91m) dash in a time of 9.4 seconds. Such was the enormity of Owens's achievement that in 2005, NBC sports commentator Bob Costas and University of Central Florida Professor of Sports History Richard C. Crepeau chose this as the most impressive athletic achievement since 1850. In 1936 Owens repeated his four gold medals haul at the NCAA Championships.

Did You Know That?
Prior to the long jump Owens placed a handkerchief 26 feet 2½ inches beyond the takeoff board, the distance of the world record, as a marker. He then jumped almost six inches past it.

❋ EL GUERROUJ FOLLOWS IN NURMI'S PATH ❋

At the 2004 Games Morocco's Hicham El Guerrouj became the first runner since Finland's Paavo Nurmi in 1924 to win the coveted double of gold medals in both the 1500 metres and the 5,000 metres.

✳ A WET BIG MAC ✳

The swim events at Los Angeles 1984 were held in the McDonald's Olympic Swim Stadium. Meanwhile, the official snack product of the Games was the Snickers bar (known as a Marathon bar in the UK).

✳ RACISTS BANNED ✳

Rome 1960 was the last Olympiad in which South Africa was allowed to participate for 32 years (until Barcelona 1992), as the IOC refused to endorse the openly racist policies of the South African government.

✳ CANADIAN TAKES ON THE USA ✳

Percy Williams of Canada was the surprise winner of both the 100 metres and the 200 metres at the 1928 Olympics in Amsterdam. Two years later Williams won the 100 metres at the inaugural British Empire Games (Commonwealth Games) held in Hamilton, Ontario. Williams's double Olympic success infuriated the Americans so much that they organized a series of indoor track meets and invited Williams to race against the best the USA had to offer. Rubbing salt into an already gaping wound, Williams won 19 of the 21 races in the series, indisputably establishing himself as the world's best sprinter at the time. Unfortunately for Williams, however, a thigh muscle injury seriously hampered his running and at the 1932 Games in Los Angeles he made it only as far as the quarter-finals. He retired from athletics and became an insurance agent.

✳ EAST GERMANY 23, USSR 22 ✳

The East German men's handball team beat the USSR 23–22 in the 1980 Olympic final to claim their first medal of any sort in the men's event.

✳ FIRST FEMALE OLYMPIC CHAMPION ✳

The first female champion of the modern Olympic Games was British tennis player Charlotte Cooper, who won the ladies' singles in Paris. She defeated the home favourite, Helene Provost, 6–1, 6–4 in the final. Cooper also won gold in the mixed doubles championships. Prior to the 1900 Games, Cooper had already won three Wimbledon ladies' singles championships (1895, 1896 & 1898) and went on to capture two more in 1901 and 1908.

❈ FOR DEMONSTRATION PURPOSES ONLY ❈

Demonstration sports were part of the Olympic Games from 1912 to 1992. Medals were awarded, but they did not count in the official tables.

Stockholm 1912......Baseball (men)
           Glima (men)
Antwerp 1920......Korfball (men)
Paris 1924......Pelota (men)
           La canne (French martial art) (men)
           Canadian canoeing and kayaking (men)
           Savate (French kickboxing) (men)
Amsterdam 1928......Kaatsen (Dutch handball) (men)
           Korfball (men) Lacrosse (men)
Los Angeles 1932......American football (men)
           Lacrosse (men)
Berlin 1936......Baseball (men)
           Gliding (men)
London 1948......Lacrosse (men)
           Swedish Ling gymnastics (men/women)
Helsinki 1952......Finnish baseball (men)
           Field handball (men)
Melbourne 1956......Australian Rules football (men)
           Baseball (men)
Rome 1960......None
Tokyo 1964......Baseball (men)
           Budo (Japanese martial art) (men)
Mexico City 1968......Pelota (men)
           Tennis (men/women)
Munich 1972......Badminton (men/women)
           Water skiing (men/women)
Montreal 1976......None
Moscow 1980......None
Los Angeles 1984......Baseball (men)
           Tennis (men/women)
Seoul 1988......Badminton (men/women)
           Baseball (men)
           Bowling (men/women)
           Judo (women)
           Taekwondo (men/women)
Barcelona 1992......Pelota (men/women)
           Roller hockey (men)
           Taekwondo (men/women)

❊ LIFE BEFORE GLORY ❊

At the first Modern Olympic Games, Athens 1896, Alfred Hajos of Hungary won both the 100 metres freestyle and the 1200 metres freestyle events. Both races were held on the same day, 11 April, and for the 1200m race the contestants were transported by boat and left to swim back to shore alone. After his 1200m victory Hajos remarked: "I must say that I shivered at the thought of what would happen if I got a cramp from the cold water. My will to live completely overcame my desire to win."

❊ PRINCESS ANNE ❊

In 1976 Princess Anne competed for Great Britain in the three-day equestrian event at the Montreal Olympics. Princess Anne once said: "The horse is about the only person who does not know you are Royal."

❊ THE DREAM TEAM ❊

Legendary basketball player Michael Jordan won two Olympic gold medals. He was part of the USA's 1984 Olympic team in Los Angeles when he was still at college, and in 1992 he was a member of the "Dream Team" at the 1992 Olympics in Barcelona. The star-studded team, which included fellow NBA legends Larry Bird, Magic Johnson, Charles Barkley, Patrick Ewing, Chris Mullin, Scottie Pippen and David Robinson, won all eight of their games in Barcelona, scoring an average of 117 points, and never took a time out.

Did You Know That?
Jordan, Ewing and Mullin are the only American players to win Olympic gold medals for men's basketball as amateurs (1984) and professionals (1992).

❊ NADIA THE CAT ❊

In the American television series *Lost*, the character Mikhail Bakunin – played by Andrew Divoff – named his cat Nadia after the multiple Olympic gold medal winner Nadia Comaneci. Bakunin referred to her as "the greatest athlete the world has ever known" and claimed he shared a birthday with the Romanian star. Comaneci was the first gymnast to successfully perform an aerial cartwheel, a double back handspring flight and an aerial walkover on the balance beam.

※ THE GAMES OF THE XVII OLYMPIAD ※

The 1960 Olympic Games were held in Rome, 52 years after Italy was forced to give up the chance to host the 1908 Games following the 1906 eruption of Mount Vesuvius. To win the right to stage the Games, Rome beat off competition from six other candidate cities: President Giovanni Gronchi officially opened the Games on 25 August 1960 in the Stadio Olimpico, Rome, with Giancarlo Peris (athletics) lighting the Olympic flame and Adolfo Consolini (athletics) performing the Olympic oath. The Games witnessed some outstanding individual performances, notably Hungary's Aladar Gerevich winning his sixth consecutive gold medal in fencing (the team sabre event), Sweden's Gert Fredriksson winning his sixth gold medal in canoeing, and Paul Elvstrom from Denmark winning a fourth consecutive gold medal in sailing. Boxer Clement "Ike" Quartey of Ghana became the first black African to win an Olympic medal when he took the silver in the light-welterweight division, and just five days later Ethiopia's Abebe Bikila won the gold medal in the marathon to become the first black African Olympic champion. Amazingly, Bikila ran the marathon barefoot. Wilma Rudolph of the USA won three gold medals in the 100 metres, the 200 metres and the 4x100m relay – a feat all the more remarkable given that she had had to overcome polio when she was a child (also she was the 20th of 22 children). Rudolph became the first American woman to win three athletics gold medals in a single Olympiad. Meanwhile, the hosts had their own hero, Sante Gaiardoni, who became the only cyclist in Olympic history to win both the time trial and the match sprint events. The closing ceremony took place on 11 September 1960. A total of 84 nations sent 5,338 athletes (4,727 men and 611 women) to participate in 150 events across 17 sports at the Games.

Rome 1960 – Final Medals Table (Top 10)

Pos.	Nation	Gold	Silver	Bronze	Total
1	USSR	43	29	31	103
2	USA	34	21	16	71
3	Italy	13	10	13	36
4	United Germany	12	19	11	42
5	Australia	8	8	6	22
6	Turkey	7	2	0	9
7	Hungary	6	8	7	21
8	Japan	4	7	7	18
9	Poland	4	6	11	21
10	Czechoslovakia	3	2	3	8

❊ GOLD FOR BRASHER AFTER APPEAL ❊

Great Britain's Chris Brasher was the first athlete across the finish line in the 3,000 metres steeplechase in Melbourne. However, to Brasher's amazement the judges disqualified him, claiming that he had interfered with Norway's Ernst Larsen, and announced Sandor Rozsnyoi of Hungary as the gold medal winner. Brasher appealed against the judges' decision and was supported in his appeal by Larsen and a few other competitors. The judges reversed their decision and Brasher became the first Briton to win a gold medal in track and field since 1932, when Thomas Hampson won the 800 metres and Thomas Green the 50km walk.

❊ A PROFITABLE GAMES ❊

Despite being held at a time when there was a worldwide economic depression, the 1932 Games in Los Angeles made a profit for the organizers of $1 million. The figure is even more remarkable when you take into account the fact that the Americans paid for the accommodation costs of the Games (they built the first Olympic Village), gave free food to all of the athletes and even paid for the entertainment of the athletes during the 16 days of events.

❊ JAPANESE HOSTS CLEAN UP ❊

The 1964 Games witnessed the appearance of two new sports, judo (men) and volleyball (men and women). Three of the four gold medals on offer in the judo weight divisions went to Japanese – Takehide Nakatani (lightweight), Isao Okano (middleweight) and Isao Inokuma (heavyweight) – while Anton Geesink of the Netherlands won the judo gold medal in the open category. In the volleyball competitions, the Soviet Union won the men's gold medal, while the women's gold went to the host nation, Japan. The women's volleyball was the first ever women's team sports event at an Olympiad.

❊ WHEN WINTER MEETS SUMMER ❊

Before the 1924 Games, it was decided, after much debate, that winter sports would be added to the Olympic Games the same year. The inaugural winter events were held in January and February, starting a tradition of holding the Winter Olympics a few months before the Summer Games, which continued until 1992.

❋ OLYMPIC TALK (14) ❋

"There can be distractions, but if you're isolated from the heart of the Games, the Olympics become just another competition."
***Mary Lou Retton**, American gymnast, 1984 Games*

❋ THE MASTER RACE ❋

During the Berlin Games of 1936, Hitler's "master race" Germany topped the medals table, winning a total of 89 medals (33 gold). The USA came second with 56 medals (24 gold).

❋ A THIRSTY GAMES ❋

Amsterdam 1928 witnessed the first appearance of Coca-Cola as a sponsor at an Olympiad. The giant American soft drinks manufacturer sponsored the entire American team with 1,000 crates of Coca-Cola, and they have been involved ever since.

❋ JESUS WINS TRIPLE HAMMER GOLD ❋

At the 1900 Games the Irish-born John "Jesus" Flanagan (representing the USA) won the hammer throw, beating fellow American Truxton Hare by 4.75 metres. Four years later, in St Louis, Flanagan successfully defended his title, defeating John DeWitt by less than one metre to set a new world record mark. At the 1908 London Games, Flanagan beat the world record holder, Matt McGrath, with his final throw to win his third consecutive hammer gold medal. On 24 July 1909, aged 41 years and 196 days, Flanagan threw the hammer 56.18 metres to become the oldest world record holder in the history of athletics. In 1911 he returned to his native Ireland, where he stayed until his death in 1938.

❋ ELEMENTARY FOR HOLMES ❋

At the 2004 Olympic Games in Athens, Great Britain's Kelly Holmes won gold medals in both the 800 metres, in a time of 1:56.38, and the 1500 metres (3:57.90).

❋ WHEN TWO BECOME ONE ❋

At the 1908 London Olympics, Australia and New Zealand were represented by a single delegation, under the name of Australasia.

Lane No./Athlete	Country	Olympic Medals
1 Tonique Williams-Darling	Bahamas	Gold – Athens 2004
2 Marie-José Perec	France	2 Gold – Barcelona 1992 & Atlanta 1996
3 Marita Koch	East Germany	Gold – Moscow 1980
4 Valerie Brisco-Hooks	USA	Gold – Los Angeles 1984
5 Cathy Freeman	Australia	Gold – Sydney 2000
6 Olga Bryzgina	USSR	Gold – Seoul 1988
7 Irena Szewinska	Poland	Gold – Montreal 1976
8 Betty Cuthbert	Australia	Gold – Tokyo 1964

❈ DORANDO PIETRI (1885–1942) ❈

Dorando Pietri was born on 16 October 1885 and grew up in Carpi, in northern Italy. The story goes that the 19-year-old Pietri saw the most famous Italian runner of the day, Pericle Pagliani, in a race held in Carpi in 1904 and, still wearing his work clothes, ran to the finish line in front of Pagliani and decided there and then to take up running. He qualified for the marathon at the Intercalated Games in Athens in 1906, but failed to finish, and in 1907 he won the Italian Championships.

When Pietri entered the White City Stadium at the end of the London Olympic marathon on 24 July 1908, everyone could see that he was in a distressed medical state. A dazed Pietri began to run in the wrong direction and then collapsed on the cinder track. Some of the officials helped him to his feet and across the finish line in first place. The USA team immediately lodged a complaint, which led to hours of arguing among the British officials and the USA team, with fights breaking out in the stands. Eventually Pietri was disqualified for receiving help and the gold medal was awarded to the American runner Johnny Hayes. However, his loss resulted in stardom for Pietri, because within minutes of his disqualification the news of what happened spread around the world. He went "from zero to hero", becoming an instant international celebrity. Queen Alexandra was so touched she gave him a gilded silver cup by way of compensation for missing out on a gold medal. Some believe that the donation of the cup was proposed by Arthur Conan Doyle (creator of the legendary character Sherlock Holmes), who was thought to be one of the officials who helped support Pietri across the finish line.

Pietri accepted an invitation to participate in exhibition races in the USA, winning 17 of the 22. On 25 November 1908, Pietri raced against Hayes in Madison Square Garden, New York, in a re-run of their Olympic encounter, and this time Pietri won fair and square. Pietri also won a second, similar race against Hayes on 15 March 1909. In May 1909, Pietri returned to his homeland and continued racing professionally in Italy and abroad for two more years. He ran his final marathon in Buenos Aires, Argentina, on 24 May 1910, setting his best ever time for the distance (2:38:48.2). The likeable Pietri lived in Sanremo, Italy, until his death of a heart attack on 7 February 1942, aged 56.

Did You Know That?
Irving Berlin, the famous composer, dedicated a song to Dorando Pietri entitled, simply, "Dorando".

※ TOP MEDAL-WINNING NATIONS ※

Year	Olympiad	Location	NOCs	Most Medals G-S-B—Total
1896	I	Athens, GRE	14	Greece (10-19-18—47)
1900	II	Paris, FRA	26	France (26-37-32—95)
1904	III	St Louis, USA	13	USA (78-84-82—244)
1906*	—	Athens, GRE	20	France (15-9-16—40)
1908	IV	London, GBR	22	Britain (54-46-38—138)
1912	V	Stockholm, SWE	28	Sweden (23-24-17—64)
1916**	VI	Berlin, GER		
1920	VII	Antwerp, BEL	29	USA (41-27-27—95)
1924	VIII	Paris, FRA	44	USA (45-27-27—99)
1928	IX	Amsterdam, NED	46	USA (22-18-16—56)
1932	X	Los Angeles, USA	37	USA (41-32-30—103)
1936	XI	Berlin, GER	49	Germany (33-26-30—89)
1940**	XII	Tokyo, JPN		
1944**	XIII	London, GBR		
1948	XIV	London, GBR	59	USA (38-27-19—84)
1952	XV	Helsinki, FIN	69	USA (40-19-17—76)
1956	XVI	Melbourne, AUS	72	USSR (37-29-32—98)
1960	XVII	Rome, ITA	83	USSR (43-29-31—103)
1964	XVIII	Tokyo, JPN	93	USSR (30-31-35—96)
1968	XIX	Mexico City, MEX	112	USA (45-28-34—107)
1972	XX	Munich, W GER	121	USSR (50-27-22—99)
1976	XXI	Montreal, CAN	92	USSR (49-41-35—125)
1980	XXII	Moscow, USSR	80	USSR (80-69-46—195)
1984	XXIII	Los Angeles, USA	140	USA (83-61-30—174)
1988	XXIV	Seoul, S KOR	159	USSR (55-31-46—132)
1992	XXV	Barcelona, SPA	169	UT*** (45-38-29—112)
1996	XXVI	Atlanta, USA	197	USA (44-32-25—101)
2000	XXVII	Sydney, AUS	199	USA (40-24-33—97)
2004	XXVIII	Athens, GRE	202	USA (35-39-29—103)

*Intercalated Games ** Games cancelled due to a World War*

*** Unified Team of 12 former USSR Republics*

※ THE GREATEST TEAM EVER ASSEMBLED ※

At the Rome Games of 1960, the greatest amateur basketball team ever assembled won the gold medal. Team USA'S 12-man squad included Oscar Robertson, Jerry West, Jerry Lucas, Walt Bellamy and Terry Dischinger, four of whom would go on to win the coveted NBA Rookie of the Year Award between 1961 and 1964.

❋ THE GAMES OF THE XVIII OLYMPIAD ❋

The Games of the XVIII Olympiad were held in Tokyo, Japan, in 1964, the first Olympics to be hosted by an Asian nation. The opening ceremony took place on 10 October 1964 and was conducted by the Emperor Hirohito. In testimony to the rebuilding of the country after the Second World War, the Olympic Flame was lit by Yoshinori Sakaï, a student born on 6 August 1945, the day the world's first atomic bomb exploded in Hiroshima. The Olympic oath was performed by Takashi Ono (gymnastics). A number of notable individual performances stood out: Dezso Gyarmati, a member of the Hungarian water polo team, won his fifth successive Olympic medal; Australia's Dawn Fraser won the 100m freestyle swimming gold medal for the third time, and the American swimmer Don Schollander won four gold medals. In athletics, Abebe Bikila of Ethiopia retained his Olympic marathon title to become the first athlete to do so. However, the star of the games was Larysa Latynina of the Soviet Union, who won two gold, two silver and two bronze medals to bring her career tally to an astonishing 18 Olympic medals. A total of 94 nations sent 5,151 athletes (4,473 men, 678 women) to participate in 163 events across 19 sports. The closing ceremony took place on 24 October 1964.

Tokyo 1964 – Final Medals Table (Top 10)

Pos.	Nation	Gold	Silver	Bronze	Total
1	USA	36	26	28	90
2	USSR	30	31	35	96
3	Japan	16	5	8	29
4	United Germany	10	22	18	50
5	Italy	10	10	7	27
6	Hungary	10	7	5	22
7	Poland	7	6	10	23
8	Australia	6	2	10	18
9	Czechoslovakia	5	6	3	14
10	Great Britain	4	12	2	18

❋ FIRST BLACK MEDAL IN THE POOL ❋

At Montreal in 1976 Enith Sijtje Maria Brigitha won two bronze medals (100m freestyle and 200m freestyle), becoming the first black swimmer to win an Olympic medal in the pool. Although she was born in Willemstad, Curacao, Brigitha represented the Netherlands at both the 1972 and 1976 Olympics.

✳ MUNICH REMEMBERED ✳

The events of the Munich Massacre (which saw 11 Israeli team members murdered at the 1972 Olympic Games) were chronicled in the Oscar-winning documentary *One Day in September*. Later they were dramatized by Steven Spielberg in his 2005 movie *Munich*. Other films made of the Munich Massacre include *Sword of Gideon*, *21 Hours At Munich* and *Munich – Mossad's Revenge*.

✳ FLAG PROBLEMS ✳

During the Parade of Nations at the opening ceremony of Stockholm 1912, the Finnish athletes paused for a few seconds to create a gap between themselves and the Russian athletes. Finland was ruled by Russia at the time, and although Russia objected to a Finnish team even being permitted to participate at the Games, they eventually agreed to this at the request of the host nation, Sweden. The Finns were still upset that they had to march under a Russian flag, and so their women's gymnastics team took out a Finnish flag as they marched into the stadium. However, it was quickly taken from the athletes by the Swedish police before the Parade of Nations passed the royal box. Things got interesting when the Finns beat their Russian rulers 2–1 in the first round of the football tournament, only to see a Russian flag being hoisted for the winning team. This also caused some confusion among the spectators, and a sign was displayed saying "Finland won". Following this, whenever a Finnish athlete won a medal at the Games a blue and white streamer (the colours of the national flag of Finland) was placed directly under the Russian flag.

✳ ONE LEG, THREE MEDALS ✳

Olivier Halassy, a member of Hungary's water polo team, won his third Olympic medal at the Berlin Games. What makes Halassy's achievement even more remarkable is that he had only one leg, the other having been amputated below the knee following a streetcar accident.

✳ MEDALS INTRODUCED ✳

The St Louis Olympics of 1904 were the first Games at which gold, silver and bronze medals were awarded to the first, second and third placed athletes.

❋ OLYMPIC TALK (15) ❋

"The Athens Olympics will be meaningful even though I cannot participate as an athlete, since I can participate in the flame relay all over the world."
Cathy Freeman, *Australian athlete, 2000 Games*

❋ THE GOLD MEDAL COLLECTOR ❋

On 16 July 1900, Raymond Clarence "Ray" Ewry of the USA won three gold medals in the standing jump events. Ewry won the standing high jump, the standing long jump and the standing triple jump. Four years later in St Louis, USA, Ewry successfully defended all three titles at the Games of the III Olympiad. Then, in London in 1908, Ewry won his third gold in the standing high jump and a third gold in the standing long jump (the standing triple jump was discontinued after 1904). If the two gold medals Ewry won at the Intercalated Games held in Athens in 1906 are included, then he won a total of 10 Olympic gold medals, making him the most successful athlete in the history of the modern Games. Ewry's world record in the standing long jump, 3.47 metres, was still standing when the event was discontinued internationally during the 1930s.

❋ SWEDEN WINS BATTLE OF THE NATIONS ❋

It is quite often the case that the nation hosting the Games finishes top of the overall medals table. In 1912 Sweden was the most successful nation, claiming 23 gold, 24 silver and 16 bronze medals. It was the first and only time that the Swedes have finished first in the "Battle of the Nations".

❋ CHINA'S TOP FEMALE ATHLETE ❋

Deng Yaping from China won four table tennis Olympic gold medals. In Barcelona 1992 she won gold in the singles competition and then partnered Hong Qiao to gold in the doubles. Four years later she retained both Olympic titles, winning a second doubles gold with Hong Qiao. Amazingly, Deng Yaping retired when she was just 24 years old, but she left her mark on the sport, having won four Olympic gold medals and 18 World Championship titles. From 1990 to 1997 she was ranked number one female player in the world, and it was no surprise when she was voted Chinese female athlete of the century.

✻ AUSSIE GOLDEN GIRL OF 1956 ✻

Betty Cuthbert of Australia won three gold medals for the host nation during the 1956 Olympics held in Melbourne (100m, 200m and 4x100m relay). Today there is a statue of the "Golden Girl" Cuthbert outside the Melbourne Cricket Ground, the stadium in which she claimed her triple gold medal haul in 1956. Eight years later in Tokyo she won gold in the 400 metres. Bobby Joe Morrow (USA) also won three gold medals at the 1956 Games, in the corresponding events in the men's competition.

✻ 2012 LOGO GIVEN THE GREEN LIGHT ✻

On 12 June 2007, the British government confirmed that it would not be asking the organizers of the 2012 Olympic Games, to be held in the capital, to change the design of their logo, despite demands for them to do so. "We believe that the new London 2012 brand will establish the character and identity of the 2012 Games, nationally and internationally, and we will not be asking the London Organizing Committee of the Olympic Games and Paralympic Games to reconsider it," said Culture spokesman Lord Davies of Oldham. The announcement followed a public outcry after a clip from the advertisement used to unveil the new logo caused a number of people in Britain who watched it to suffer an epileptic seizure. "You must at least concede one fact. The purpose of a logo is to identify and bring to everyone's attention the brand in question. This brand has certainly drawn the nation's attention," said Lord Davies. However, he did add that the government shared the concerns of those people who suffer from epilepsy, adding: "It wasn't the logo itself. It was the video." Lord Stoddart of Swindon, an Independent Labour peer, asked: "Why did it cost £400,000 to produce such an uninspiring logo?" to which Lord Davies replied: "It may be uninspiring to some and inspiring to others."

✻ THE FIRST OLYMPIC VILLAGE ✻

At Los Angeles in 1932 the male athletes were housed in a single Olympic Village for the first time. It was purpose built in Baldwin Hills, a suburb of Los Angeles, and covered 321 acres (130 hectares). The male athletes were housed in some 550 bungalows, and there was a hospital, a library, a post office and 40 kitchens serving a variety of food to cater for all tastes. The female athletes stayed in a luxury hotel, the Chapman Park Hotel on Wilshire Boulevard, Los Angeles.

❋ THE OLYMPIC MOTTO ❋

The Olympic motto is *Citius, Altius, Fortius,* which is Latin for Faster (or swifter), Higher, Stronger. The motto was proposed in 1894 by Baron Pierre de Coubertin, the founder of the modern Olympic Games, at the meeting in Paris which established the International Olympic Committee. De Coubertin borrowed the saying from his friend Henri Didon, a Dominican priest who himself was an athletics fanatic. The words are believed to have been engraved on the main entrance of the stadium where the ancient Olympic Games were held. The motto was also the name of an Olympic history journal from 1992 until 1997, when it was renamed the *Journal of Olympic History.*

❋ OLYMPIC TORCH VISITS LONDON IN 2008 ❋

In keeping with tradition, the Olympic Torch went through London on its way from Mount Olympia in Greece to Beijing in China for the 2008 Games. The Torch was lit – using the rays of the Sun – on 25 March 2008, arrived London in early April, then travelled through Europe, South America and Asia, including a leg in the foothills of Mount Everest, before arriving in Beijing in July 2008. The torch relay always includes a visit to the city staging the Games four years hence to stir up local interest. In 2008, around 20,000 torchbearers covered approximately 137,000 km (85,125 miles) on the relay.

❋ BEN'S SAILING TREBLE ❋

British sailor Ben Ainslie, OBE, won the silver medal at Atlanta 1996 in the Laser class, the gold medal at Sydney 2000 also in the Laser class, and a second gold medal at Athens 2004 in the Finn class.

❋ FAIR PLAY BRIT ❋

In the final of the women's individual foil at Los Angeles, British fencer Helen Seymour Guinness ended her own hopes of claiming a gold medal in the event when she informed the officials that they had not scored two touches against her by her opponent, Ellen Preis of Austria.

❋ SPACE GAMES ❋

The Tokyo Olympics of 1964 were telecast to the USA using Syncom 3, the first ever geostationary communication satellite, and it was the first television programme to cross the Pacific Ocean.

❋ SEVEN GOLDS FOR THE BIG RED ❋

Nikolai Andrianov of the USSR won four gold medals in men's gymnastics in Montreal, including the prestigious all-around title, floor exercise, rings and vault. Four years earlier he won gold in Munich in the floor exercise and when Moscow played host to the 1980 Olympics, he won two more gold medals (team and vault). He also won eight other Olympic medals, five silver and three bronze.

❋ A ROWING PHENONEMON ❋

Vyacheslav Nikolayevich Ivanov of the Soviet Union won the gold medal in the rowing single sculls at the 1964 Olympics in Tokyo, adding to the golds he won in the same event at the 1956 and 1960 Olympics. In 1962 he won the inaugural World Rowing Championships, and in addition to his triple Olympic gold medal haul he won the USSR single scull championship in 11 consecutive years (1956–66) and the European Rowing Championships four times (1956, 1959, 1961 & 1964).

❋ THE BLOOD IN THE WATER MATCH ❋

The water polo final rounds match between Hungary and the Soviet Union at the 1956 Olympic Games is considered to be the most infamous water polo match in history and is known as "the Blood in the Water match". Just as the athletes set off for the Games in November 1956, the Hungarian Revolution started and was instantly crushed by the might of the Soviet army. Many of the Hungarian athletes vowed never to return home to be ruled by the Soviets and saw their match in the pool as a means of fighting back. Germany, Hungary, Italy, Soviet Union, USA and Yugoslavia all qualified from their groups for the final rounds matches. With only two games left to play for each team, the Hungarians led the table, a single point ahead of Yugoslavia and two points clear of the Soviet Union. With two points awarded for a win, the Soviets knew that victory over Hungary would draw them level at the top of the table. The Hungary versus Soviet Union match turned into a blood-bath as fighting broke out in the pool. With a minute remaining and the Hungarians leading 4–0 the game had to be stopped to prevent angry Hungarians in the crowd reacting to Valentin Prokopov's punch on Ervin Zador, which caused blood to pour from the Hungarian's badly split eye. The Hungarians defeated Yugoslavia 2–1 in their final match to claim the gold medal.

※ THE GAMES OF THE XIX OLYMPIAD ※

The Games held in Mexico City proved to be the most controversial Olympiad to date. As soon as Mexico City won the right to host the Games many NOCs raised concerns about the safety of their athletes. The city is situated 7,349 feet (2,300m) above sea level and the air contains 30 per cent less oxygen than at sea level. The 1968 Games took place in the context of the Vietnam War, the assassinations of Martin Luther King and Robert Kennedy and the USSR's invasion of Czechoslovakia. Just 10 days before the opening ceremony 260 Mexico City university students were killed by troops. When the Games finally got under way on 12 October 1968, after the opening ceremony had been performed by President Gustavo Diaz Ordaz in the Estadio Olímpico Universitario, the rarefied air, although unfriendly to endurance athletes, assisted many others in breaking world records. Indeed, every one of the men's races at 400m or less, plus the men's and women's relays, the long jump and triple jump all witnessed new world records. Bob Beamon's (USA) leap of 8.90 metres in the long jump survived for 22 years. Norma Enriqueta Basilio de Sotelo, a Mexican hurdler, became the first woman to light the Olympic flame, and sex testing for women was introduced for the first time at an Olympiad. However, the Games will always be remembered for the acts of two athletes, Tommie Smith and John Carlos, two black Americans who, after winning the gold and bronze medals respectively in the 200 metres, bowed their heads and gave the Black Power salute during the playing of the USA national anthem as a protest against racism in their country. A total of 112 nations sent 5,516 athletes (4,735 men, 781 women) to participate in 172 events across 20 sports. The closing ceremony took place on 27 October 1968.

Mexico 1968 – Final Medals Table (Top 10)

Pos.	Nation	Gold	Silver	Bronze	Total
1	USA	45	28	34	107
2	USSR	29	32	30	91
3	Japan	11	7	7	25
4	Hungary	10	10	12	32
5	East Germany	9	9	7	25
6	France	7	3	5	15
7	Czechoslovakia	7	2	4	13
8	West Germany	5	11	10	26
9	Australia	5	7	5	17
10	Great Britain	5	5	3	13

※ 1936 OLYMPIC TORCH ※

At the opening of the Games the Olympic flame was lit by a flame that originated from the fire at the sanctuary of the ancient Olympic Games in Olympia. This was the first time in the history of the modern Games that this had occurred, and every Olympiad since has followed this method. During the 1934 Session, the IOC agreed to the proposal made by the Secretary-General of the Berlin Games organizing committee for athletes to carry the flame in relay from Olympia to Berlin. The IOC consulted with the NOCs of the six countries the flame would have to pass through (Greece, Bulgaria, Yugoslavia, Hungary, Austria and Czechoslovakia) and they all unanimously supported the idea and agreed that the route planned should include each capital city. The torch itself was made from polished steel and designed by the sculptor, Lemcke. The handle of the torch was inscribed *Fackelstaffel-Lauf Olympia-Berlin* 1936 ("1936 Berlin Olympics Torch Relay") and had the five Olympic rings and the German eagle superimposed on it; on the lower section of the torch the flame's route from Olympia to Berlin (a total journey of more than 3,000km) was set out.

※ MARATHON DISTANCE ESTABLISHED ※

For the 1924 Games, the distance of the marathon was fixed at 42.195 kilometres, the same distance run at the 1908 Olympics held in London. Finland's Albin Stenroos won the 1924 Olympic marathon.

※ IOC MEMBER CLAIMS GOLD ※

Otto Herschmann won a silver medal as a member of the Austrian team in the team sabre fencing event. At the time Herschmann was president of the Austrian Olympic Committee. He remains the only sitting National Olympic Committee president to win a medal at an Olympic Games.

※ NOT SO HAPPPY GAMES ※

The official slogan of the 1972 Munich Olympics was "the Happy Games", and the official emblem of the Games was a blue solar logo (the "Bright Sun"). However, the murder of 11 Israeli athletes by Arab terrorists during the Olympiad cast one of the darkest shadows in sports history over the Games.

✳ FIRST PARTICIPATING NATIONS ✳

A total of 14 different nations were represented at the Athens Games of 1896:

Australia ✤ Austria ✤ Bulgaria ✤ Chile ✤ Denmark
France ✤ Germany ✤ Great Britain ✤ Greece – host nation
Hungary ✤ Italy ✤ Sweden ✤ Switzerland ✤ USA

Belgium and Russia entered the names of competitors but later withdrew them.

✳ LOGO ATHLETE ✳

At the 1976 Olympic Games in Montreal, Finland's Lasse Viren retained both his 5,000m and 10,000m titles. After winning the 10,000 metres he removed his track shoes and waved them in the air to the crowd on his victory lap. The IOC accused the Finn of blatant advertising, as the logo of the shoe manufacturer could be clearly seen on the soles of his shoes. However, Viren protested his innocence, claiming that he removed the shoes as he had a blister. But the IOC suspended him from taking place in the 5,000 metres final after he qualified from his heats. Viren and the Finnish team lodged an appeal and he was readmitted to the race just two hours before the starting gun was fired.

✳ YIFTER THE SHIFTER ✳

Miruts Yifter's talent for long-distance running was first noticed when he joined the Ethiopian Air Force. He was called up to the Ethiopian national team for the 1968 Olympics held in Mexico City, but only made his debut at an Olympiad four years later in Munich, where he won a bronze medal in the 10,000 metres. Miruts missed the 1976 Olympiad in Montreal, when Ethiopia was among the African countries boycotting the Games. However, at the 1980 Olympiad in Moscow, Miruts won double gold in the 5,000 metres and 10,000 metres, emulating Lasse Viren's (Finland) athletics 5,000m and 10,000m double in the 1972 and 1976 Olympiads. As a result of his ability to change his speed during a race Yifter was nicknamed "Yifter the Shifter". At the Moscow Games much controversy surrounded Yifter's age, which was reported to be between 33 and 42. However, Miruts blatantly refused to give a definitive answer, and when questioned on the subject by reporters he said: "Men may steal my chickens; men may steal my sheep. But no man can steal my age."

❈ OLYMPIC TALK (16) ❈

"It's at the borders of pain and suffering that the men are separated from the boys."
*Czechoslovakia's greatest long-distance runner, **Emil Zatopek**, a man indeed*

❈ FALLING OVER THE LINE ❈

When Switzerland's Gabrielle Andersen-Scheiss staggered into the Los Angeles Coliseum at the end of the women's marathon she was clearly suffering from heat exhaustion, but the medical team on hand allowed her to continue. It took her more than five minutes to complete the final 400 metres before she eventually fell across the finish line.

❈ BIONDI'S SEVEN-UP ❈

US swimmer Matt Biondi won seven medals at the 1988 Games. He claimed five gold medals, in the 50m individual freestyle, 100m individual freestyle, 4x100m freestyle relay, 4x200m freestyle relay and 4x100m medley relay, a silver in the 100m individual butterfly, and a bronze in the 200m individual freestyle. Biondi had also won a gold medal at the Los Angeles Olympics in 1984 (in the 4x100m freestyle relay). At Barcelona in 1992 he took two more gold medals (4x100m freestyle relay and 4x100m medley relay) and a silver in the 50m individual freestyle. Overall, Biondi won 11 medals, eight gold, two silver and one bronze.

❈ FANS BOO WINNER ❈

Finland's Lauri Lehtinen won the gold medal in the men's 5,000 metres in Los Angeles. However, Lehtinen was lucky not to have been disqualified by the officials after he twice blocked US runner Ralph Hill as the pair raced down the final straight. When the Finn crossed the line first the American spectators booed, but they were soon silenced when the stadium announcer, Bill Henry, uttered the words: "Remember, please, these people are our guests."

❈ FIRST OLYMPIC BOYCOTT ❈

The IOC invited the Soviet Union to participate in the 1948 London Games, but they declined the invitation.

✳ FANTASY MEN'S 800M OLYMPIC FINAL ✳

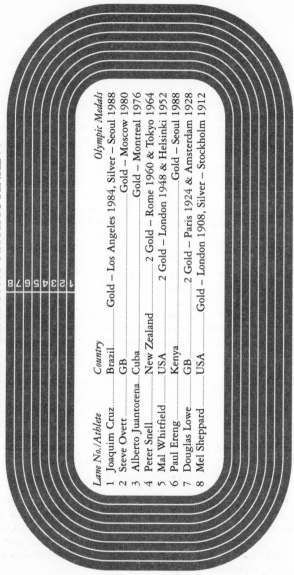

Lane No./Athlete	Country	Olympic Medals
1 Joaquim Cruz	Brazil	Gold – Los Angeles 1984, Silver – Seoul 1988
2 Steve Ovett	GB	Gold – Moscow 1980
3 Alberto Juantorena	Cuba	Gold – Montreal 1976
4 Peter Snell	New Zealand	2 Gold – Rome 1960 & Tokyo 1964
5 Mal Whitfield	USA	2 Gold – London 1948 & Helsinki 1952
6 Paul Ereng	Kenya	Gold – Seoul 1988
7 Douglas Lowe	GB	2 Gold – Paris 1924 & Amsterdam 1928
8 Mel Sheppard	USA	Gold – London 1908, Silver – Stockholm 1912

❋ THAI GOLD ❋

At Athens Pawina Thongsuk became the first female from Thailand to win an Olympic gold medal, the 75kg category in weightlifting. She lifted 122.5kg in the snatch and produced a new Olympic record lift of 150kg in the clean and jerk for a combined score of 272.5kg.

❋ MEDALS IN SUMMER AND WINTER GAMES ❋

East Germany's Christa Luding-Rothenburger made Olympic history at the 1988 Summer Games in Seoul. She won the silver medal in the 1,000 metres cycling individual sprint race to add to two medals she had won a few months earlier in speed skating (gold in the 1,000 metres and silver in the 500 metres) during the 1988 Winter Games in Calgary. This made her the only person in history to win winter and summer medals in the same year and one of only a few athletes ever to win medals in both the Summer and Winter Games.

❋ RICH GAMES ❋

Los Angeles 1984 was the first Olympiad since 1896 (Athens) to be hosted without government financing, but it still managed to make a profit of $223m. It was only the second time that an Olympiad had made a profit, the previous occasion being the 1932 Games – also hosted by Los Angeles. *Time* magazine was so impressed with the financial success of the Games that it named the organizer, Peter Ueberroth, its "Man of the Year".

❋ BATHROOM GOLD MEDAL ❋

Don Thompson of Great Britain won the gold medal in the 50km walk during the 1960 Games. Thomson acclimatized to the Italian heat by training in his bathroom, which he sealed and kept hot with steam kettles and heaters.

❋ TARZAN IN THE MONEY ❋

After his swimming career ended, Johnny Weissmuller (winner of five Olympic gold medals in 1924 & 1928) was invited for a screen test for the role of Tarzan and was chosen ahead of 150 other applicants. In a total of 12 Tarzan movies, Weissmuller earned an estimated $2 million and established himself as the best known of all the actors who have ever portrayed the legendary "Lord of the Jungle".

✳ THE GAMES OF THE XX OLYMPIAD ✳

The 1972 Munich Games will be remembered for two events: Mark Spitz's incredible haul of seven gold medals in the pool, setting seven world records along the way, and the murder of 11 Israeli athletes by the Black September terrorist organization. The Games of the XX Olympiad saw archery reintroduced to the Olympic programme after an absence of 52 years and handball after 36. The 1972 Olympics also saw the introduction of the first ever named Olympic mascot, a dachshund called Waldi. Liselott Linsenhoff of West Germany sent the home crowd into a frenzy when she became the first female equestrian to win a gold medal in an individual event (the dressage).

The Games also saw a 17-year-old Soviet gymnast named Olga Korbut win three gold medals and a silver medal. In the pentathlon, 33-year-old Mary Peters of Great Britain set a new world record on her way to becoming the new "golden girl of British athletics" by winning the gold medal. The opening ceremony took place in Munich's Olympiastadion on 26 August 1972 and was conducted by President Gustave Heinemann, while the Olympic flame was lit by Gunter Zahn (athletics, junior 1500m champion). Heidi Schüller (athletics) performed the Olympic oath, and the first ever officials' oath was performed by Heinz Pollay (equestrian sports). A total of 121 nations sent 7,134 athletes (6,075 men, 1,059 women) to participate in 195 events across 23 sports.

Munich 1972 – Final Medals Table (Top 10)

Pos.	Nation	Gold	Silver	Bronze	Total
1	Soviet Union	50	27	22	99
2	USA	33	31	30	94
3	East Germany	20	23	23	66
4	West Germany	13	11	16	40
5	Japan	13	8	8	29
6	Australia	8	7	2	17
7	Poland	7	5	9	21
8	Hungary	6	13	16	35
9	Bulgaria	6	10	5	21
10	Italy	5	3	10	18

✳ HUNGARY FOR SUCCESS ✳

Rudolf Bauer, the Hungarian discus thrower, was the only non-American gold medallist in the field events at the 1900 Games.

❀ OLYMPIC TALK (17) ❀

"An Olympic medal is the greatest achievement and honour that can be received by an athlete. I would swap any world title to have won gold at the Olympics."
Jeff Fenech, Australian boxer, 1984 Games

❀ BRITISH LONG JUMP DOUBLE ❀

At the 1964 Tokyo Olympics Great Britain claimed the long jump double gold, with Lynn Davies winning the men's event and Mary Rand the women's.

❀ GOLD FOR GOULD ❀

Although Mark Spitz (USA) was unquestionably the dominant athlete at the 1972 Olympics, winning seven gold medals in the pool and establishing a new world record in each of the seven events he entered, the achievements of 15-year-old Australian swimmer Shane Gould did not go unnoticed. Gould picked up three gold medals in the pool, winning the 200m and 400m freestyle and the 200m individual medley, setting a new world record each time. She also added a silver medal in the 800m and a bronze medal in the 100m freestyle. Gould is the only person, male or female, to hold every world record in the freestyle events from 100m to 1500m simultaneously, and the first female swimmer ever to win three Olympic gold medals in new world record times. Not long after the Munich Games she retired from the sport, aged just 16.

❀ BREAKING THE GENDER BARRIER ❀

During the 1928 Amsterdam Olympics Poland's Halina Konopacka won a gold medal in the discus throw, the first Olympic gold medal ever won in a women's track and field event.

❀ KING AND QUEEN OF THE COURT ❀

At the 1996 Atlanta Games Andre Agassi (USA) won the tennis gold medal in the men's singles event. His win helped him become the first male player ever to win the career Golden Slam, clinched in 1999 when he finally won the French Open singles title. Interestingly, Steffi Graf, who later married Andre, was the first female player to win the Golden Slam, striking Olympic gold in Seoul in 1988.

✳ FANNY BLANKERS-KOEN (1918–2004) ✳

Francina ("Fanny") Blankers-Koen was born Francina Elsje Koen on 26 April 1918 in Lage Vuursche, near Baarn, in the Netherlands. When she was growing up Koen enjoyed a number of sports including fencing, gymnastics, ice skating, swimming and tennis. In 1935, aged 17, Fanny took up competitive athletics and in what was only her third competitive race she set a national record in the 800m and was chosen for the Dutch Olympic team to attend the 1936 Berlin Olympics. However, as the 800m had been removed from the women's Olympic calendar after 1928, she joined the sprint team and was selected for the 4x100m relay and the high jump.

At the Berlin Olympics, both her events took place on the same day, and she could manage only a fifth-place finish in each. In 1938 Fanny set her first world record, running the 100 yards in 11.0 seconds, but World War Two put paid to her Olympic medal hopes for nine years. At the 1948 London Olympics Fanny entered the 100m, the 200m, the 80m hurdles and the 4×100m relay (she had to drop the high jump and the long jump as IOC rules stipulated that an athlete could not compete in more than three individual track and field events). Before the Games many people questioned her ability to succeed, given that she was a 30-year-old mother of two, and Jack Crump, the British team manager, said she was "too old to make the grade". There were also cries from the Netherlands for her to stay at home and look after her children instead of competing in athletics events.

At the 1948 Games her first event was the 100m, which she won easily, thus becoming the first Dutch athlete to win an Olympic title in track and field. In the 80m hurdles she was up against Great Britain's Maureen Gardner, who ironically was also coached by Fanny's husband, Jan Blankers. In a thrilling final Fanny claimed the gold medal in a photo finish (11.2 seconds). Fanny then won the inaugural women's 200m Olympic gold medal in a time of 24.4 seconds, before claiming her fourth gold as a member of the 4x100m relay team. The very same people who criticized her decision to compete welcomed her home a national hero, while those who questioned her ability were left to regret their words. During her career, Fanny set or tied 12 world records in eight different events – 100 yards, 100m, 200m, high hurdles, high jump, long jump, pentathlon, and 4x110 yard relay.

Did You Know That?
Fanny Blankers-Koen also won a total of 58 national championships and five European titles.

❋ OLYMPIC TALK (18) ❋

"The Olympics have been with the world since 776 BC, and have only been interrupted by war, especially in the modern era."
***Bill Toomey**, American decathlete, 1968 Games*

❋ LONDON'S TREBLE ❋

The 2012 Summer Olympic Games, the Games of the XXX Olympiad, will take place in London from 27 July 2012 to 12 August 2012. London won the right to host the Games following a bidding process which took place on 6 July 2005. London will become the first city to host three Olympiads.

Did You Know That?
Birmingham and Manchester have both bid unsuccessfully to host the Olympics.

❋ MARATHON WINNER AFTER JUST 9 MILES ❋

After just nine miles of the marathon in the 1904 Summer Olympics, US runner Frederick Lorz was totally exhausted and decided he could not complete the gruelling 26 miles in temperatures in the nineties. His manager then gave him a lift in his car for the next 12 miles until the car broke down at the side of the road. Lorz continued on foot back to the Olympic stadium to collect his clothes, and when he crossed the finish line the race officials thought he was the winner of the race. He then played along with the idea that he was the Olympic marathon champion and was ready to accept the gold medal. The assembled press even took photographs of President Roosevelt's daughter, Alice, placing a laurel wreath over Lorz's head. However, just before the medal presentation an official said that he had seen Lorz passing the halfway mark of the race in a car, and Lorz finally came clean and admitted that it was a joke. The American Athletics Union (AAU) did not see the funny side of Lorz's joke and banned him from the sport for life. In 1905 the AAU reinstated Lorz and he won the Boston Marathon the same year.

❋ GERMANY AND JAPAN NOT INVITED ❋

With the events of the Second World War still fresh in the memory, the IOC did not invite Germany or Japan to participate in the 1948 London Olympics.

❋ WITH BOW AND RACQUET ❋

The London Games of 1908 saw archers William and Charlotte "Lottie" Dod become the first brother and sister medallists at an Olympic Games. Both are descendants of Sir Anthony Dod of Edge, who commanded the British archers at the Battle of Agincourt. William won gold in the men's Double York round while Lottie took silver in the women's Double National round. Amazingly the brother and sister had not taken up competitive archery until 1906 when they moved home from Cheshire to Berkshire. However, Lottie was best known as a tennis player, winning the Wimbledon Ladies Singles Championships five times. When she won her first Wimbledon crown in 1887 she was only 15 years old, and she remains the youngest player to win the Ladies' Singles tournament (Martina Hingis was three days younger when she won the Women's Doubles title in 1996). In addition to archery and tennis, Lottie competed in many other sports including field hockey and golf. She won the British Ladies Amateur Golf Championship (in 1904 at Royal Troon) and represented the England Women's National Field Hockey Team (which she helped to found). *The Guinness Book of Records* named her as the most versatile female athlete of all time, along with Babe Zaharias of the USA (athletics and golf).

❋ FIRST ASIAN INDIVIDUAL GOLD ❋

At Amsterdam Japan's Mikio Oda won the triple jump with a leap of 15.21 metres to become the first Asian to claim a gold medal in an individual event. At the Amsterdam Games, Oda also competed in the long jump and finished seventh in the high jump. In 1931 Oda set a new world record of 15.58 metres in the triple jump while he was a student at Waseda University, Japan. Oda died on 2 December 1998, aged 93, and in 2000 a panel of track and field experts voted him the Male Asian Athlete of the Century.

❋ FOUR GOLD MEDALS FOR *PLAYGIRL* PIN-UP ❋

At Seoul in 1988 US diver Greg Louganis struck his head on the springboard while attempting a reverse 2½ pike during the qualifying round for the 3-metre springboard event. In the final he won the gold medal to retain his Olympic title, and he also retained his Olympic title in the 10-metre platform event. In 1987 Greg posed nude in *Playgirl* magazine, and in 1994 he informed the world that he was gay.

✳ THE BARON CLAIMS THE SILVER ✳

Great Britain's rowing eight were coxed to silver medal success at the 1980 Olympics by Colin Moynihan (the 4th Baron Moynihan). On 5 October 2005, the former MP and Minister for Sport was elected Chairman of the British Olympic Association (BOA), beating the 1968 Mexico City Olympic 400m hurdles champion David Hemery by 28 votes to 15.

✳ BUDD AND DECKER CLASH ✳

During the women's 3,000 metres final at the 1984 Olympics, Zola Budd (GB) appeared to cut in front of the home favourite, Mary Decker, causing the American athlete to stumble and fall on to the infield and out of the race. The crowd went mad with fury, even though the barefooted Budd finished out of the medal places back in seventh place. The American team filed a protest and Budd was disqualified from the race. The decision was later overturned when the video evidence proved that Budd had not done anything wrong.

✳ 1976 AFRICAN BOYCOTT ✳

The 1976 Games were boycotted by African countries following the IOC's refusal to ban New Zealand from the Olympiad. New Zealand's national rugby team (the All Blacks) had continued to play Rugby Union matches with South Africa, a country banned from the Olympics since 1964 because of its apartheid policies. The following 28 countries boycotted the Games:

Algeria ✳ Cameroon ✳ Central African Republic ✳ Chad
Congo ✳ Egypt ✳ Ethiopia ✳ Gabon ✳ Gambia ✳ Ghana
Guyana ✳ Iraq ✳ Kenya ✳ Libya ✳ Madagascar ✳ Malawi ✳ Mali
Morocco ✳ Niger ✳ Nigeria ✳ Sudan ✳ Swaziland ✳ Tanzania
Togo ✳ Tunisia ✳ Uganda ✳ Upper Volta ✳ Zambia

✳ BOY HELPS ROWERS TO GOLD ✳

During the rowing competition at the Paris Games the Dutch coxed pair was missing a coxswain. On 26 August 1900, a French boy was chosen from the crowd and the Dutch pair rowed to Olympic glory. The young boy, believed to be no more than 10 years old, joined in the Dutch rowing team's victory ceremony and even had his photograph taken. To this day no one knows his name or what age he really was.

❋ THE GAMES OF THE XXI OLYMPIAD ❋

The Games of the XXI Olympiad were held in Montreal, Canada, in 1976 and were the most expensive in history. On 17 July 1976, HRH Queen Elizabeth II (as the Head of State of Canada) officially opened the Olympiad, and two young athletes, Stephane Prefontaine and Sandra Henderson (aged 16 and 15, respectively), lit the Olympic flame. The Olympic oath was performed by Pierre Saint-Jean (weightlifting) and the officials' oath by Maurice Forget (athletics). Despite the Games being the subject of a boycott by African nations, a number of outstanding individual performances stood out. The star of the Games was a 14-year-old gymnast from Romania named Nadia Comaneci, who caught the attention of the world when she was awarded the first ever perfect 10.00 for her performance on the uneven bars (she went on to record six more perfect scores at the Games). In volleyball, the Japanese women's team won all their matches in straight sets (only one nation reached double figures against them in a game). Poland's Irena Szewinska won the 400 metres to bring her wonderful career to an end at the Olympiad, having amassed seven Olympic medals (three gold, two silver, two bronze) in five different events (100m, 200m, 400m, 4x100m and the long jump). A total of 92 nations sent 6,084 athletes (4,824 men, 1,260 women) to participate in 198 events across 21 sports at the Games. The closing ceremony took place on 1 August 1976.

Montreal 1976 – Final Medals Table (Top 10)

Pos.	Nation	Gold	Silver	Bronze	Total
1	USSR	49	41	35	125
2	East Germany	40	25	25	90
3	USA	34	35	25	94
4	West Germany	10	12	17	39
5	Japan	9	6	10	25
6	Poland	7	6	13	26
7	Bulgaria	6	9	7	22
8	Cuba	6	4	3	13
9	Romania	4	9	14	27
10	Hungary	4	5	13	22

❋ ATHLETES BOOED ❋

During the track and field events at the Moscow Games some athletes complained about the crowd's booing of competitors from East Germany and Poland.

❊ SMOKIN' JOE ❊

Joe Frazier of the USA won the heavyweight boxing gold medal at the 1964 Olympics. In 1967 Muhammad Ali (gold medal winner in the heavyweight division at the 1960 Olympics) was stripped of his world heavyweight boxing championship belt after he refused to enlist in the US Army, objecting to the war in Vietnam. The following year Frazier fought Buster Mathis for the vacant title and won it with a knockout of his opponent in the 11th round. During his career Frazier fought Ali three times, winning their first encounter in 1971 but losing the following two in 1974 and 1975.

❊ TIME-LAG GAMES ❊

The Games of Rome 1960 were broadcast live by more than 100 television channels worldwide including, with a time-lag, the USA, Canada and Japan. CBS, an American television network, paid the IOC $394,000 for the right to broadcast the Games.

❊ A ROWING SUCCESS ❊

At the 1936 Games, Great Britain's Jack Beresford set a record by winning his fifth Olympic medal. The British rower had won a gold medal in the single sculls in 1924, gold again in the coxless fours in 1932, silver in the single sculls in 1920, and silver in the eights in 1928. In Berlin he added his fifth medal, and his third gold, in the double sculls.

❊ TURNAROUND GAMES ❊

At Sydney in 2000 the US softball team lost three games in a row before turning their Games around and defeating each of the teams they had lost to as they went on to win the gold medal.

❊ LATE START FOR THE 100 METRES ❊

In Paris Great Britain's Harold Abrahams won the gold medal in the 100 metres as well as a silver medal in the 4x100m relay. In the 100 metres final, held at 7 p.m. on 7 July 1924, Abrahams beat the 1920 Olympic champion, Charlie Paddock of the USA, into silver medal position, with New Zealand's Arthur Porritt winning the bronze. Abrahams and Porritt dined together at 7 p.m. on 7 July every year thereafter, until Abrahams's death in 1978.

❈ OLYMPIC TALK (19) ❈

"Hard work has made it easy. That is my secret. That is why I win"
*Nadia Comaneci, Romanian gymnast who recorded the first ever perfect
10.00 scores in Olympic gymnastic history in Montreal, 1976*

❈ OLYMPIC FLAME GOES OUT ❈

A few days after the Olympic flame was lit at the opening
ceremony of the 1976 Olympics held in Montreal, Canada, a
rainstorm put it out. An official relit the flame using his cigarette
lighter but, in keeping with tradition, the Games' organizers
put it out again and this time relit it using a back-up flame
taken from the original ceremonial flame at Olympia. When the
Olympic flame arrived in the Panathinaiko Stadium in Athens
to start the torch relay ahead of the 2004 Athens Olympics,
a wind blew out the flame of the Olympic torch. However,
Gianna Angelopoulous-Daskalaki, a member of the Athens 2004
organizing committee, quickly relit it with the back-up flame
from Olympia.

❈ LOST OLYMPIADS ❈

The games of three Olympiads have been lost as a result of the two
World Wars:

Olympiad	Host City	Year
VI	Berlin	1916
XII	Helsinki	1940
XIII	London	1944

Did You Know That?
Helsinki's Olympiastadion was a purpose-built stadium for the XII
Olympiad. It finally played host in 1952 (XV Olympiad).

❈ SIX TEAMS, THREE STATES, ONE WINNER ❈

Field hockey made its inaugural Olympic appearance at the London
Games. A total of six teams entered from three states: the United
Kingdom of Great Britain and Ireland was represented by a team
from each of the four home nations, Germany was represented by a
club team, and France sent a team comprised of players from three
different clubs. England won the gold medal, with Ireland claiming
silver and Wales taking bronze.

❈ REDGRAVE'S SPORTING MOMENT ❈

In 2002 Steve Redgrave's achievement of winning his fifth consecutive gold medal at an Olympic Games (1984–2000) was voted the greatest sporting moment in Channel 4's *100 Greatest Sporting Moments*.

❈ THE WORLD'S STRONGEST MAN ❈

Vasily Ivanovich Alekseyev of the USSR is generally considered to be the greatest super-heavyweight weightlifter of all time. In 1970 Alekseyev set his first world record, and from 1970 to 1977 he was undefeated in his class, winning every World Championship and European Championship title during his eight-year reign. He won the gold medal at the 1972 Munich Olympics and retained his championship four years later in Montreal. However, at the 1980 Moscow Olympics he set his opening weight too high and after three unsuccessful attempts he was eliminated from the competition. He retired from weightlifting after the Moscow Games but his legacy remains: he was the first man to lift in excess of 600kg in the triple event and he set 80 world records and 81 Soviet records during his career.

Did You Know That?
Alekseyev coached the Russian Unified weightlifting team at the 1992 Olympics in Barcelona, where they won 10 medals, five of them gold.

❈ SORRY, NO MORE GOLD ❈

Stockholm 1912 was the last Games at which solid gold medals were awarded. Today the winners' medals are usually gold-coated silver.

❈ KNOCKED-OVER GOLD ❈

Robert ("Bob") Morton Newburgh Tisdall from Ireland won the gold medal in the 400 metres hurdles at the 1932 Olympics in a new world record time of 51.7 seconds. Because of an IOC rule existing at the time, however, his record time could not be validated as he had hit a hurdle on his way to victory. Subsequently the rules for the event were changed. When Juan Antonio Samaranch became the President of the IOC in 1980 he presented Tisdall with a Waterford crystal bowl with the image of him knocking over the last hurdle engraved into the glass.

❋ AN AMERICAN HEROINE ❋

America found a new heroine at Atlanta and she came in the diminutive shape of 18-year-old Kerri Strug from Tucson, Arizona. The American ladies gymnastics team were determined to break Russia's stranglehold on the team competition and to win the gold medal for the first time in their history. The eyes of the world were fixed on the competition, which went into its final day with the Russians holding a narrow lead. However, in front of a packed 40,000 audience inside the Georgia Dome on 23 July 1996 the US team put on a majestic display and their Russian counterparts could only sit back and watch their lead gradually slip away. In the final rotation the American girls had already notched up enough points to claim the gold medal, but those on the floor believed that the USA team still required a single good score on the vault to win the gold medal. Dominique Moceanu (USA) fell on both of her vaults and recorded low scores, and so it was left to Strug, who was the last to vault for the USA. However, Kerri suffered the same fate as her team-mate, falling on her first vault, and as she got back to her feet she shook her ankle which she had hurt in the fall. Kerri limped to the end of the runway in preparation for her second attempt. What followed will never be forgotten by those in the Dome or the millions watching live on television – an Olympic moment that will live for ever. Kerri landed her vault perfectly on one foot, raised her arms to salute the mesmerized judges and then hopped around to raise her arms once more to salute the ecstatic crowd before collapsing in agony on to the mat, holding her damaged ankle. The judges awarded her a score of 9.712 and with it the gold medal for the USA. Her coach, the legendary Bela Karolyi, carried her on to the podium to join her team-mates for the medal ceremony, after which she was taken to hospital, where it was discovered that she had suffered two torn ligaments in her ankle. As a result of her injury Strug had to withdraw from the individual all-around competition and floor finals, two events in which she reached the finals. After the Games she became a national celebrity and was even invited to the White House to meet President Bill Clinton.

❋ JAPANESE MASTERY ❋

The 1964 Olympics gave Japan a world stage on which to display its talent for organization. The Games were so successful that the IOC awarded Japan three awards: the Olympic Cup, the Bonacossa Trophy and the "Diploma of Merit".

❊ CHILLY EVENT ❊

The Athens Games of 1896 saw the first ever Olympic swimming contests, which were held in the Bay of Zea. The water temperature was a chilly 13 degrees Celsius.

❊ THE HERO FROM PRAGUE ❊

Just two months before the 1968 Olympics opened, the Soviet Union invaded Czechoslovakia. After the invasion Vera Caslavska, a Czech gymnast, went into hiding before attending the Olympiad. At the Games the brave woman from Prague won four gold medals (individual all-round, vault, uneven bars and – in a tie for first place – the floor) and two silvers (beam and team). Caslavska married Josef Odlozil, winner of the 1964 Olympic 1500m silver medal, in Mexico City shortly after the 1968 Games ended. At the 1960 Olympics in Rome Caslavska won a silver medal in the team event and in the 1964 Tokyo Games she won three golds (individual all-around, vault and beam) and one silver (team).

❊ TRIPLE DIVING GOLD ❊

In 1976 when Klaus Dibiasi of Italy won his third consecutive Olympic platform diving gold medal, he became the first to achieve this feat in a diving event. His 1968 gold had already made him the first Italian to become an Olympic champion in a diving event, and his 1976 medal made him the first diver to be awarded medals in four Olympiads.

❊ RUGBY ENTERS THE OLYMPICS ❊

Rugby made its first appearance at an Olympiad at the Paris Games of 1900, but only three teams entered. A French representative side defeated Moseley Wanderers from England and a German side from Frankfurt to be crowned Olympic champions. Remarkably, the Moseley team played a full game of rugby in England the day before they left for Paris by train and boat. They arrived in Paris the following morning, played the French side that afternoon and were back in England by the next morning. Consequently the scheduled game between Moseley and Frankfurt was cancelled, and both teams were awarded the silver medal. Gold medals were not awarded at the Games of the II Olympiad, Paris 1900. The winners received silver medals, and bronze medals were awarded to the runners-up.

❈ THE GAMES OF THE XXII OLYMPIAD ❈

A USA-led boycott of the Moscow Olympics in 1980 reduced the number of participating nations to 80, the lowest number since Melbourne 1956 (72). The calls for a boycott, in which President Jimmy Carter of the USA was the principal voice, stemmed from widespread disapproval of the USSR's invasion of Afghanistan in December 1979. In the end 65 nations boycotted the Games, including West Germany, Canada, China and Japan. However, the Games went ahead as scheduled, with the opening ceremony taking place on 19 July 1980 in the Luzhniki Stadium, with President Leonid Brezhnev in attendance. The lighting of the Olympic flame was performed by Sergei Belov (basketball), the Olympic oath was delivered by Nikolay Andrianov (gymnastics) and the officials' oath by Aleksandr Medved (wrestling).

The Games witnessed some outstanding individual performances, notably those of Soviet gymnast Aleksandr Dityatin, who won a medal in all eight men's gymnastics events to become the only athlete ever to win eight medals at a single Olympiad; Cuba's Teofilo Stevenson, who won his third successive super-heavyweight gold medal to become the first boxer to win the same division three times; and, in track and field, Gerd Wessig of East Germany, who became the first male high jumper to break the world record during an Olympic Games, jumping 2.36 metres (7 feet 9 inches). Amazingly, Wessig qualified for the team only two weeks before the start of the Games. A total of 5,179 athletes (4,064 men, 1,115 women) participated in 203 events across 21 sports at the Games. The closing ceremony took place on 3 August 1980 and during the closing ceremony, Misha the bear cub (the mascot of the 1980 Moscow Games), appeared with a tear dropping from an eye.

Moscow 1980 – Final Medals Table (Top 10)

Pos.	Nation	Gold	Silver	Bronze	Total
1	USSR	80	69	46	195
2	East Germany	47	37	42	126
3	Bulgaria	8	16	17	41
4	Cuba	8	7	5	20
5	Italy	8	3	4	15
6	Hungary	7	10	15	32
7	Romania	6	6	13	25
8	France	6	5	3	14
9	Great Britain	5	7	9	21
10	Poland	3	14	15	32

✼ COXLESS PAIRS DOUBLE TAKE ✼

Both the gold and silver medal winning rowing teams in the coxless pairs event at the Moscow Games were identical twins. East German twins Bernd and Jorg Landvoigt took the gold medal, while Nikolai and Yuri Pimenov of the USSR claimed the silver. Great Britain's Malcolm Carmichael and Charles Wiggin finished in the bronze medal position.

✼ WEIGHTLIFTING LIGHTWEIGHTS ✼

The Soviet-led boycott of the Los Angeles Olympics had a bigger effect on weightlifting at the Games than on any other sport. No fewer than 94 of the top 100 ranked lifters in the world, 29 of the 30 medallists from the last World Weightlifting Championships and all 10 of the defending Olympic Champions from Moscow 1980 (five from the USSR, two from Cuba, one from Bulgaria and one from Czechoslovakia) stayed at home. At the 1984 Olympics the gold medals in the 10 weight categories were won by China (4), Romania (2), West Germany (2), Australia (1) and Italy (1).

✼ DECATHLON FIRST ✼

Boxing, dumbbells, freestyle wrestling and the decathlon all made their Olympic debut at the 1904 St Louis Games. They were all passed at the 1901 IOC Session held in Paris.

✼ A BED OF ROSES ✼

Michel Theato, who was described as a French gardener, won the marathon at the 1900 Games in a time of 2 hours, 59 minutes and 45 seconds. Theato crossed the winning line more than 40 minutes ahead of his nearest competitor, Sweden's Ernest Fast. Meanwhile, US runner Richard Grant, who finished sixth in the marathon, complained to the race officials that a cyclist had knocked him down just as he was about to run past Theato. Other competitors claimed that Theato had taken a shortcut during the marathon, pointing out that if he had run the proper course he would have been mud-splattered like them. Theato was certainly a dark horse in one respect. When he crossed the finishing line a military band played "La Marseillaise", but it has since been discovered that he was born in Luxembourg and maintained his Luxembourgian citizenship throughout his life.

✳ FANTASY WOMEN'S 800M OLYMPIC FINAL ✳

12345678

Lane No./Athlete	Country	Olympic Medals
1 Doina Melinte	Romania	Gold – Los Angeles 1984
2 Nadezhda Olizarenko	Soviet Union	Gold – Moscow 1980
3 Ellen van Langen	Netherlands	Gold – Barcelona 1992
4 Maria Mutola	Mozambique	Gold – Sydney 2000, Bronze – Atlanta 1996
5 Sigrun Wodars	East Germany	Gold – Seoul 1988
6 Ann Packer	Great Britain	Gold – Tokyo 1964
7 Tatyana Kazankina	Soviet Union	Gold – Montreal 1976
8 Kelly Holmes	Great Britain	Gold – Athens 2004, Bronze – Sydney 2000

OLYMPIC STADIA

Olympics	*Stadium*
1896 Athens	Panathinaiko Stadio
1900 Paris	Vélodrome de Vincennes
1904 St Louis	Francis Field
1908 London	White City Stadium
1912 Stockholm	Stockholms Olympiastadion
1920 Antwerp	Olympisch Stadion
1924 Paris	Stade Olympique de Colombes
1928 Amsterdam	Olympisch Stadion
1932 Los Angeles	Los Angeles Memorial Coliseum
1936 Berlin	Olympiastadion
1948 London	Wembley Stadium
1952 Helsinki	Olympiastadion
1956 Melbourne	Melbourne Cricket Ground
1960 Rome	Stadio Olimpico
1964 Tokyo	National Olympic Stadium
1968 Mexico City	Estadio Olímpico Universitario
1972 Munich	Olympiastadion
1976 Montreal	Le Stade Olympique
1980 Moscow	Lenin Stadium
1984 Los Angeles	Los Angeles Memorial Coliseum
1988 Seoul	Jamsil Olympic Stadium
1992 Barcelona	Estadi Olímpic de Montjuic
1996 Atlanta	Centennial Olympic Stadium
2000 Sydney	Stadium Australia
2004 Athens	Olympiako Stadio Athinas "Spyros Louis"
2008 Beijing	Beijing National Stadium
2012 London	Olympic Stadium

Did You Know That?

The 1928 Amsterdam Olympisch Stadion, designed by Jan Wils, won the gold medal in architecture at the 1928 Olympics.

ALL ABOARD

In 1912 the concept of an Olympic Village was still some years away. The teams stayed in small hotels or rented rooms all over Stockholm, while the USA team stayed on board the transatlantic liner in which they had arrived.

OLYMPIC TALK (20)

"The Olympics remain the most compelling search for excellence that exists in sport, and maybe in life itself."

***Dawn Fraser**, Australian swimmer, three times Olympic gold medallist*

❋ MARK SPITZ (1950–) ❋

Mark Andrew Spitz was born on 10 February 1950 in Modesto, California. In 1952 his family moved to Hawaii, where he learned how to swim, before returning to live in Sacramento, California, four years later. At the age of six he was competing in local swimming events, and at nine he started training at Arden Hills Swim Club, Sacramento. However, he then had a difficult decision to make: to continue with his Hebrew education or to concentrate on swimming. His father encouraged him to continue swimming, and at the age of 10 he held 17 national records and one world record for his age group and was named as the world's best under-11 swimmer. A 16-year-old Spitz won the 100m butterfly at the National AAU Championships, the first of his 24 AAU titles. Then, in 1967, he took home five gold medals from the Pan-American Games in Winnipeg, Canada. Mark entered his first Olympiad in Mexico City in 1968, and prior to the Games a confident Spitz, who had already set 10 world records, openly stated that he would return home with six gold medals. However, he was left to rue his brashness when he could only finish second in the 100m butterfly, third in the 100m freestyle and last in the 200m butterfly. To spare his blushes he did win two team gold medals in the 4x100m freestyle and the 4x200m freestyle. In order to focus on the 1972 Olympics, to be held in Munich, Spitz dedicated every available minute to swimming and won eight individual NCAA titles. He was named World Swimmer of the Year in 1969, 1971 and 1972 and also won the Sullivan Award in 1971 as the country's top amateur athlete.

At the 1972 Munich Olympics Spitz set his goal on winning the six gold medals he predicted he would win four years earlier. In fact he went one better and won a staggering seven, claiming the 100m freestyle (51.22), 200m freestyle (1:52.78), 100m butterfly (54.27), 200m butterfly (2:00.70), 4x100m freestyle (3:26.42), 4x200m freestyle (7:35.78) and the 4x100m medley (3:48.16). What was even more remarkable about his "Magnificent Seven" gold medal haul was the fact that Spitz set a new world record in each of the seven events he entered. His feat remains unequalled by any other athlete in a single Olympiad. Between 1968 and 1972, Spitz won nine Olympic gold medals, as well as one silver and one bronze.

Did You Know That?
Mark also won 5 Pan-American gold medals, 31 National US Amateur Athletic Union titles, and eight US National Collegiate Athletic Association Championships, and he set 33 world records in the process.

❉ COFFEE TIME FOR THE ATHLETES ❉

Brazil sent a total of 69 athletes to Los Angeles, but only 24 of them actually competed in the Games. As with many nations at the time, the worldwide economic depression placed a huge financial burden on Brazil and the only way the Brazilian NOC could get the team to Los Angeles was to put them on a barge along with 25 tons of coffee. The idea was to stop off at various ports en route and sell the coffee to pay for the athletes' expenses. However, they managed to sell only US$24 worth of coffee, and at the time the USA required each person entering the country to pay US$1 head tax, which meant that 45 athletes were left on board the barge. However, the Brazilian consulate in San Francisco soon learned of the plight of the 45 athletes and sent a courier to Los Angeles with a cheque made out in Brazilian cruzeiros to the value of US$45. However, by the time the courier arrived the Brazilian cruzeiro had devalued so much that the cheque was now only worth US$17. To make matters worse, the cheque bounced when it was presented for payment.

❉ OWN GOALS FOR COE AND OVETT ❉

At Moscow in 1980 Steve Ovett (GB) won the gold medal in the 800 metres (his less favoured event), while Sebastian Coe (GB) had to settle for the silver medal. In the 1500 metres final Coe won gold, while Ovett could manage only a bronze in what was his best distance.

❉ FINNEGAN'S GOLD ❉

Great Britain's Chris Finnegan won the gold medal in the middleweight boxing division at the 1968 Games. He defeated Alexey Kiselev of the USSR on a 3–2 majority points decision in the final.

❉ WHITE LIGHTNING STRIKES GOLD ❉

In Montreal Cuba's Alberto Juantorena, nicknamed "White Lightning", became the first athlete to win both the 400 metres and the 800 metres at an Olympiad. Juantorena won the 800m gold medal in a new world record time of 1:43.50, and three days later he claimed the 400m gold in a low-altitude world record time of 44.26 seconds. Four years earlier, in Munich, Juantorena was eliminated in the semi-finals of the 400 metres, and in the same event at the 1980 Moscow Olympics he finished fourth.

❋ THE GAMES OF THE XXIII OLYMPIAD ❋

The Games of the XXIII Olympiad were held in Los Angeles in 1984. The city had played host to the Games half a century earlier in 1932, but on this occasion there were no other candidates to host them. Four years after the USA led a boycott of the 1980 Moscow Olympics, the Russians exacted their revenge by leading a boycott of the 1984 Games. Thirteen communist bloc allies of the Soviet Union stayed away, the only Warsaw Pact country to participate being Romania (winners of a national record of 53 medals). However, despite the communist snub, a record 140 nations took part. Carl Lewis (USA) was the indisputable star of the Games, winning four gold medals and thereby equalling the feat of Jesse Owens (USA) at the 1936 Olympics held in Berlin. The Games also witnessed a number of firsts: Joan Benoit (USA) won the inaugural women's marathon; Connie Carpenter-Phinney (USA) claimed the gold medal in the first women's cycling road race; Sebastian Coe (GB) retained his 1500m title (the first athlete to do so excluding the Intercalated Games of 1906), and Neroli Fairhall was the first paraplegic athlete to take part in a medal event when she competed in the archery competition from her wheelchair. Rhythmic gymnastics, synchronized swimming and wind surfing also made their first appearance at an Olympiad. On 28 July 1984, the Games were officially opened by President Ronald Reagan, and the Olympic flame was lit by Rafer Johnson (decathlete). The Olympic oath was performed by Edwin Moses (athletics) and the officials' oath by Sharon Weber (gymnastics). A total of 6,829 athletes (5,263 men, 1,566 women) participated in 221 events across 23 sports. The Games attracted 9,190 media personnel (4,863 broadcasters and 4,327 journalists), while 28,742 volunteers helped the Olympiad run smoothly. The closing ceremony took place on 12 August 1984.

Los Angeles 1984 – Final Medal Table (Top 10)

Pos.	*Nation*	*Gold*	*Silver*	*Bronze*	*Total*
1	USA	83	61	30	174
2	Romania	20	16	17	53
3	East Germany	17	19	23	59
4	P.R. of China	15	8	9	32
5	Italy	14	6	12	32
6	Canada	10	18	16	44
7	Japan	10	8	14	32
8	New Zealand	8	1	2	11
9	Yugoslavia	7	4	7	18
10	South Korea	6	6	7	19

✻ ROYAL FAMILY MOVE MARATHON START ✻

The official marathon distance of 26 miles and 385 yards (42.195km) from the start to the finish line inside the stadium was established at the London Games of 1908. Originally the marathon covered a distance of 26 miles, but in 1908 a further 365 yards were added at the beginning of the race in order that the royal family could obtain a good view of the start from the balcony at Windsor Castle. This distance became official from the 1924 Games onwards.

✻ A HUNGRY ATHLETE ✻

Among the more unusual entrants to the marathon at St Louis in 1904 was a Cuban postman named Felix Caravajal. He had raised the funds to get to the Games by running around the central square in Havana and stopping between laps to appeal for contributions to his Olympic fund, shouting to passers-by from a soap box. However, having finally raised the money he needed to travel to St Louis he then proceeded to lose it en route to the Olympics in a crap game in New Orleans. When he arrived in the stadium the officials had to postpone the start of the marathon for several minutes while Caravajal cut the sleeves off his shirt and the legs off his pants. He did not own any training shoes, and so had to run the race in lightweight street shoes. During the race he stopped along the route to chat with bystanders, and when he got hungry he stole some peaches from a race official. He then deviated from the marathon route to eat some green apples from a nearby orchard. However, later in the 26-mile race he developed stomach cramps and had to drop out for a time. Eventually Felix rejoined the race and managed to finish fourth overall.

✻ BLACK PROTEST OR CASUAL BEHAVIOUR? ✻

In the final of the 400 metres in Munich, Vincent Matthews from the USA won the gold medal, and his team-mate Wayne Collett claimed the silver medal. When the two black American athletes stood on the podium for the medal ceremony they could be seen joking with each other and twirling their medals. The IOC did not take too kindly to their actions, likening them to the Black Power protest performed by their fellow black Americans Tommie Smith and John Carlos at the 1968 Olympics in Mexico City. Although the pair protested their innocence, the IOC banned them from any future Olympiads. Following their ban the USA had to withdraw from the 4x400m relay race as they did not have runners to take part.

❋ OLYMPIC TALK (21) ❋

"The last 15 metres were very difficult."
Eric Moussambani, "Eric the Eel", the swimmer from Equatorial
Guinea whose time in the 100 metres freestyle at the 2000 Olympic Games
in Sydney was 1:52.72, slower than the 200m world record, and 50
seconds slower than any other competitor in the event

❋ THE ANCIENT OLYMPIC GAMES ❋

Some historians claim the Ancient Games began in Olympia, Greece
in 776 BC and were celebrated until AD 393. However, many myths
and legends are attributed to the origin of the ancient Olympic
Games. One such myth claims that Zeus initiated the Games after
his defeat of the Titan Cronus. Another legend claims that Heracles,
the son of Zeus, was the creator of the ancient Games and built the
Olympic stadium and surrounding buildings as a tribute to his father.
Some historians attribute the ancient Games to Pelops, the mythical
King of Olympia and eponymous hero of the Peloponnesus, claiming
that the Christian Clement of Alexandria made offerings to Pelops
during the Games: "The Olympian games are nothing else than the
funeral sacrifices of Pelops." And yet another myth tells of King
Iphitos of Elis who is said to have consulted the Pythia (the Oracle of
Delphi) in an attempt to prevent a war being waged against his people
by the Spartans in the ninth century BC. The story goes that King
Iphitos was advised by the Prophetess to organize a series of games in
honour of the gods, and that his Spartan opponent decided to stop the
war during these games, which were called Olympic, and named after
the sanctuary of Olympia where they were held. The Games were held
every four years and the period between two Games became known as
an "Olympiad", a method used by the Greeks to count years.

❋ FENCING CHEAT ❋

During the 1976 Montreal Olympics Boris Onischenko, a member
of the USSR's modern pentathlon team, was disqualified after judges
discovered that he had rigged his epee to register a hit against an
opponent when one had not taken place. As a direct result of the
Russian's blatant cheating the entire USSR modern pentathlon
team was kicked out of the competition. Onischenko's actions were
so despised by the Russian Olympic team that the USSR's men's
volleyball team threatened to throw him out of a window at the
team's hotel if they ran into him.

※ ATHLETES GREETED FROM OUTER SPACE ※

During the opening ceremony in Moscow, the crew of the Salyut 6 Space Station, Leonid Popov and Valery Ryumin, sent their best wishes to the athletes via a live satellite link-up between the Station and the Central Lenin Stadium. The cosmonauts appeared on the stadium's scoreboard.

※ AN ABORIGINAL GOLD ※

Ten days after Cathy Freeman lit the Olympic flame at the opening ceremony, the Aboriginal Australian won the 400 metres final before an ecstatic home crowd in the Telstra Stadium. Freeman's win made her the first athlete in the history of the Olympic Games to light the Olympic flame and then go on to win a gold medal at the same Games.

※ A TRUNCHEON FOR A HAMMER ※

Matt McGrath, an Irish-American policeman, first competed in the Olympic hammer event at St Louis in 1904 (he was the reigning world record holder at the time). At the Games of the IV Olympiad, London 1908, he was beaten in the hammer final by another Irish-American policeman, the defending Olympic champion John Flanagan. However, at the 1912 Stockholm Olympics McGrath finally claimed gold. In 1920 McGrath attempted to defend his hammer title in Antwerp, but injured his knee and had to withdraw after his second throw, taking fifth place. At the Paris Games of 1924, two decades after his Olympic debut, McGrath won the silver medal, aged 45.

※ TOO DRUNK TO COMPETE ※

The Games of 1968 witnessed the first drug disqualification when Hans-Gunnar Liljenwall, a Swedish entrant in the modern pentathlon, tested positive for excessive alcohol.

※ THE FIRST LOST OLYMPIAD ※

The Stockholm Games were closed on 27 July with a banquet at Restaurant Hasselbacken. There Baron Pierre de Coubertin gave a hopeful speech about the future of the Games and how the IOC was very much looking forward to the next Olympiad, to be held in Berlin in 1916. However, almost exactly two years later, on 28 July 1914, the First World War began and the 1916 Olympics were cancelled.

✻ WILKIE HALTS DOMINANT AMERICANS ✻

At Montreal in 1976, the USA men's swimming team was so dominant that they won a staggering 12 of the 13 gold medals on offer in the pool. Amazingly, they also won 10 silver medals and five bronze medals, making a total of 27 medals from the 39 available. The only man to prevent the USA from claiming a clean sweep of the gold medals was Great Britain's David Wilkie, who won the 200 metres breaststroke in a new world record time of 2:19.20. Wilkie also claimed a silver medal for the 100 metres backstroke.

✻ 12 GREAT DISPLAYS WITHOUT A MEDAL ✻

During the 1980 Moscow Games, 12 track and field athletes performed so well that their scores would have won the gold medal at any previous Olympiad. However, in Moscow they all went home without a medal to their names. Amazingly, for the first time in Olympic history all eight male participants in the long jump final exceeded the 8 metre mark, while in the women's long jump three athletes jumped 23 feet for the first time ever in one competition.

✻ FORGOTTEN SPORTS ✻

At the 1894 Sorbonne congress, when Athens was chosen to host the inaugural Olympic Games of the modern era in 1896, many different sports were scheduled for the Games. When the first edition of the official programme advertising the Games was published, cricket and football were included as competitions. However, neither of these came to fruition in Athens in 1896. Rowing was included in the original programme but was cancelled on the day of the competition as a result of strong winds, and the yachting competition did not take place either. According to the official report from the Games the yachting had to be cancelled because "we had no proper boats for this, nor did any foreign ones appear for the contest".

✻ OUTSTANDING OLYMPIC RECORDS ✻

Going into the 2008 Olympics in Beijing, China, three Olympic records set during the 1980 Moscow Olympics remain unbeaten: the East German Ilona Slupianek's shot put of 22.41 metres, the East German women's 4x100 metres relay time of 41.6 seconds and the 1:53.43 set by Soviet athlete Nadezhda Olizarenko in the 800 metres.

❊ GB'S FOREIGN GOLD WINNER ❊

In 1908 Serbia and Montenegro were not members of the International Olympic Committee. However, their first athlete to win a gold medal did so at the London Olympics. Paul Radmilovic was a member of the Great Britain water polo team that claimed gold in these Games. He also won a gold medal as a member of Great Britain's 4x200m freestyle relay team in 1908. Nicknamed "Pavao", he also won gold medals in water polo at the Olympics in Stockholm (1912) and in Antwerp (1920).

❊ BROTHERS IN ARMS ❊

Rafer Johnson of the USA won the decathlon gold medal in Rome, with Yang Chuan-Kwang of the Republic of China claiming the silver medal and the USSR's Vasili Kuznetsov the bronze. Johnson and Yang were decathlon training partners at the University of California at Los Angeles (UCLA), and following the final event the two athletes embraced and leaned against each other, completely exhausted.

❊ THE MASTER FENCER ❊

In 1912 the 18-year-old Nedo Nadi of Italy won the individual foil fencing gold medal at the Stockholm Olympics. In the First World War he was decorated by the Italian government for bravery shown while fighting for his country. During the Antwerp Games of 1920 Nadi won five fencing gold medals using three different weapons. First of all he helped Italy win the team foil gold, and then he secured the gold medal in the individual foil (winning 22 matches and losing just two). His third gold at the 1920 Games came in the team epee event, and he followed this up a few days later claiming gold medals in the individual and team sabre for a record five fencing medals at the same Games. His brother, Aldo, also won a gold medal in each of the three team events, and after the VII Olympiad he taught as a professional in South America. When he returned to his homeland a few years later his amateur status was restored and he was appointed the president of the Italian Fencing Federation. Nedo's father, Beppe, did not approve of the epee, which he considered to be an "undisciplined" weapon, so the young Nadi would sneak out of the family home and practise with it elsewhere. His insubordination paid off when he won a gold medal in the team epee event in Antwerp.

✳ THE GAMES OF THE XXIV OLYMPIAD ✳

The Games of the XXIV Olympiad were held in Seoul, South Korea. The city had won the right to host the 1988 Olympics back in 1981, seeing off the rival bid from Nagoya (Japan), and South Korea was only the second Asian nation to host an Olympiad, following Tokyo in 1964. The Democratic People's Republic of Korea (North Korea), technically still at war with South Korea, boycotted the Games when the IOC refused their demands to be co-hosts of the Olympiad. Cuba, Ethiopia and Nicaragua supported North Korea by staying at home. The main talking-point from the Games was the disqualification of Canada's Ben Johnson after he won the men's 100 metres final in a world record time of 9.79 seconds but failed a drugs test. He was also expelled from the Games in disgrace.

On 17 September 1988, the Games were officially opened by President Roh Tae-woo, and the Olympic flame was lit by Chong Son-man, Kim Won-tak and Son Mi-jong (athletics). In an emotional moment at the opening ceremony the Olympic torch was run into the stadium by 76-year-old Sohn Kee-chung, the winner of the 1936 Olympic marathon in Berlin who was forced to compete for Japan as Korea was occupied by the Japanese at the time. The Olympic oath was performed by Hur Jae (basketball) and Son Mi-na (handball), and the officials' oath was taken by Lee Hak-rae (judo). A total of 159 nations sent 8,391 athletes (6,197 men, 2,194 women) to compete in 237 events across 25 sports at the Games; and 52 nations won medals at the Games, 31 of them taking home gold medals. The closing ceremony took place on 2 October 1988. A total of 27,221 volunteers helped out at the Seoul Olympics, and 11,331 media personnel (6,353 broadcasters and 4,978 journalists) reported the stories from the Olympiad to the world.

Seoul 1988 – Final Medals Table (Top 10)

Pos.	Nation	Gold	Silver	Bronze	Total
1	USSR	55	31	46	132
2	East Germany	37	35	30	102
3	USA	36	31	27	94
4	South Korea	12	10	11	33
5	West Germany	11	14	15	40
6	Hungary	11	6	6	23
7	Bulgaria	10	12	13	35
8	Romania	7	11	6	24
9	France	6	4	6	16
10	Italy	6	4	4	14

❊ ONE IN TEN ❊

At the 1968 Olympics in Mexico City, Mark Spitz (USA), winner of two gold medals, finished second in the final of the 100 metres butterfly to his team-mate Doug Russell. It was the first time in 10 races that Spitz had lost to Russell. Four years later, in Munich, Spitz entered seven events and won a further seven gold medals.

❊ VICTORY BY 1/100 OF A SECOND ❊

British swimmer Adrian Moorhouse won the gold medal in the 100 metres breaststroke in Seoul in a time of 1:02.04, just one-hundredth of a second ahead of Hungary's Karoly Guttler (1:02.05), with Dimitry Volkov (USSR) third in 1:02:20. Moorhouse's arch rival, Victor Davis of Canada, could only finish fourth. Davis won gold in the 200 metres breaststroke in Los Angeles 1984, but died in November 1989 when he was struck by a car outside a nightclub in Sainte-Anne-de-Bellevue, a suburb of Montreal. He was only 25 years old.

❊ THE RIGHT ANGLE ❊

US wrestler Kurt Angle won the gold medal in the freestyle wrestling heavyweight (90–100kg) division despite suffering a fractured neck. After the Olympiad, Angle went on to star in Vince McMahon's World Wrestling Entertainment (WWE) and won the WWE Championship belt four times and the World Heavyweight Championship belt once. He remains the only professional wrestler to have won an Olympic gold medal.

❊ NBC SPLASH-OUT ❊

NBC Universal paid the IOC $793 million for the US broadcast rights to the 2004 Athens Olympics, the highest fee paid by any country.

❊ FROM THE POOL TO THE OFFICE ❊

Great Britain's Duncan Goodhew won the 100m breaststroke gold medal at the 1980 Olympics and added a bronze in the 4x100m medley relay event. Duncan has alopecia universalis (a total lack of body hair), which writers claimed gave him a small advantage over his competitors in the pool as it made him more hydrodynamic.

❄ OLYMPIC TALK (22) ❄

"And there goes [Alberto] Juantorena down the back straight, opening his legs and showing his class."
*BBC TV commentator and athletics coach, **Ron Pickering**, watches Cuba's 400m and 800m gold medallist accelerate at the 1976 Games in Montreal*

❄ FIRST WINTER EVENTS HELD ❄

The Olympic Games of 1908 were the first to include winter events. Four figure skating events were contested but held months apart from most of the other events.

❄ VIETNAMESE DELIGHT ❄

Taekwondo was introduced as a medal sport in 2000, and in the competition Vietnam won its first ever Olympic medal – having begun competing in the Olympics in 1952. Hieu Ngan Tran won the silver medal in the women's 49–57kg category.

❄ FIRST ALL-ROUND ATHLETE ❄

At the 1896 Games, Carl Schumann from Germany won three events in gymnastics (individual horse vault and horizontal bar and parallel bars team competitions). He also won the Greco-Roman wrestling tournament and competed in three events in athletics (long jump, triple jump and shot put) plus the weightlifting competition.

❄ GOLDEN PUNCH-UP ❄

Hungarian swimmer Zoltan Halmay won the 100 metres and 50 metres freestyle at St Louis in 1904. However, when Halmay beat the home favourite, the USA's J. Scott Leary, by just one foot in the 50m event, the American judge awarded the gold medal to Leary. The ruling culminated in a fight between the two swimmers, whereupon the judges ordered a rematch. Halmay won the re-run race to claim gold for his country.

❄ FIRST OLYMPIC VILLAGE ❄

The concept of a designated Olympic Village for the athletes did not come to fruition until the 1932 Summer Olympics, held in Los Angeles. Prior to these Games all athletes had to cater for their own lodging.

❋ INAUGURAL FAIR PLAY AWARD ❋

The 1964 Games witnessed the presentation of the IOC's inaugural "Fair Play Award". In the regatta race the Swedish pair of Lars Gunnar Kall and Stig Lennart Kall gave up their chances of winning the gold medal when they stopped to help two fellow competitors whose boat had sunk.

❋ FIRST MUSLIM GOLD ❋

When Nawal El Moutawakel (Morocco) won the inaugural women's 400m hurdles gold medal at the 1984 Games, she became the first Muslim and first African female Olympic champion. She was also the first Moroccan athlete of either sex to win a gold medal at an Olympiad.

❋ OLYMPIC EMBARRASSMENT ❋

One of the most embarrassing moments in Olympic history came at St Louis in 1904. The organizers decided to hold "Anthropology Days". As the Games also formed part of the Louisiana Purchase Exposition (the 1904 World's Fair), a number of indigenous men from all over the world were in St Louis. Unbelievably, competitions were held to see how these indigenous men fared against white men on level terms. Events such as mud fighting, rock throwing, pole climbing and spear throwing were part of the farce.

❋ MEDALS CEREMONY ❋

At the first ten Olympic Games of the modern era the medals were presented at the closing ceremony of each Olympiad. However, at Los Angeles in 1932 each medal ceremony took place shortly after the event had reached its conclusion, a tradition that was adopted at subsequent Olympiads and became a permanent feature.

❋ THE GOLDEN BOYS ❋

Great Britain's 4x100m relay team won the gold medal at the Athens Olympics of 2004 in a time of 38.07 seconds. The golden quad comprised Jason Gardener, Darren Campbell, Marlon Devonish and Mark Lewis-Francis. The highly fancied USA team had to settle for the silver medal, while Nigeria claimed an unexpected but very welcome bronze medal.

❋ INTERNATIONAL OLYMPIC COMMITTEE (2007) ❋

There are currently 111 IOC members, 25 honorary members and two honour members (Kurt Furgler of Switzerland and Henry Kissinger of the USA). Juan Antonio Samaranch is Honorary President for life.

President

Jacques Rogge .... Belgium

Vice-Presidents

Gunilla Lindberg .... Sweden
Lambis V. Nikolaou .... Greece
Chiharu Igaya .... Japan
Thomas Bach .... Germany

Members

Gerhard Heiberg .... Norway
Denis Oswald .... Switzerland
Mario Vázquez Raña .... Mexico
Ottavio Cinquanta .... Italy
Sergey Bubka .... Ukraine
Zaiqing Yu .... People's Republic of China
Richard L. Carrión .... Puerto Rico
Ser Miang Ng .... Singapore
Mario Pescante .... Italy
Sam Ramsamy .... South Africa

Address:
Executive Board, Château de Vidy
1007 Lausanne, Switzerland

❋ SPITZ EXONERATED ❋

After receiving the gold medal in the 200m freestyle medal ceremony Mark Spitz waved his track shoes to salute the cheering crowd. There were accusations of commercialism, led by the USSR, but Spitz was found innocent by the IOC.

❋ GRECO-SWEDISH SPORTSMANSHIP ❋

In the true spirit of sportsmanship, the final in the middleweight category of Greco-Roman wrestling at the London Olympics in 1908, between two Swedes, Frithiof Martensson and Mauritz Andersson, was postponed one day to allow Martensson to recover from a minor injury. Martensson eventually won the gold medal.

✳ FANTASY MEN'S 1500M OLYMPIC FINAL ✳

Lane No./Athlete	Country	Olympic Medals
1 Jim Lightbody	USA	2 Gold – St Louis 1904 & Athens 1906*
2 Paavo Nurmi	Finland	Gold – Paris 1924
3 Sebastian Coe	GB	2 Gold – Moscow 1980 & Los Angeles 1984
4 Noureddine Morceli	Algeria	Gold – Atlanta 1996
5 Peter Rono	Kenya	Gold – Seoul 1988
6 Hicham El Guerrouj	Morocco	Gold – Athens 2004
7 Kipchoge Keino	Kenya	Gold – Mexico City 1968
8 Peter Snell	New Zealand	Gold – Tokyo 1964

* *Intercalated Games*

❋ THE GAMES OF THE XXV OLYMPIAD ❋

The Games of the XXV Olympiad, held in Barcelona in 1992, saw all of the IOC countries participating for the first time since the 1972 Olympics in Munich. Even South Africa, which had been excluded from the Olympic family for 32 years on account of its Apartheid policy, was now invited back into the fold. These were also the first Summer Olympics since the reunification of East and West Germany in 1990, as well as the reunification of North and South Yemen. The Germans competed as a unified team for the first time since the 1960 Olympics in Rome. The Baltic states of Estonia and Latvia took part in an Olympics as individual nations for the first time since the 1936 Games in Berlin, while Lithuania made their first appearance since 1928 (Amsterdam). The remaining 12 former Soviet Republics formed a Unified Team (although the medal winners were permitted to use the flags of their own Republics). In the former Yugoslavia, Croatia, Bosnia & Herzegovina and Slovenia all sent athletes representing these nations for the first time in Olympic history. Yugoslav athletes could not compete under their flag or in team events, but were allowed to compete under the Olympic banner as independent Olympic participants. The opening ceremony took place on 25 July 1992 in the Lluis Companys Olympic Stadium, where the Games were officially opened by HRH King Juan Carlos I. Antonio Rebollo (paralympic archer) lit the Olympic flame by firing an arrow over the top of the Olympic cauldron, igniting gas that was released from it. The Olympic oath was performed by Luis Doreste Blanco (sailing) and the officials' oath by Eugeni Asencio (water polo). A total of 169 nations sent 9,356 athletes (6,652 men, 2,704 women) to compete in 257 events across 28 sports. The closing ceremony took place on 9 August 1992. A total of 34,548 volunteers were in attendance along with 13,082 media (7,951 broadcasters, 5,131 journalists).

Barcelona 1992 – Final Medals Table (Top 10)

Pos.	Nation	Gold	Silver	Bronze	Total
1	Unified Team (ex-USSR)	45	38	29	112
2	USA	37	34	37	108
3	Germany	33	21	28	82
4	China	16	22	16	54
5	Cuba	14	6	11	31
6	Spain	13	7	2	22
7	South Korea	12	5	12	29
8	Hungary	11	12	7	30
9	France	8	5	16	29
10	Australia	7	9	11	27

✳ 2012 LOGO UNVEILED ✳

On 4 June 2007, the logo for "the Games of the London 2012 Olympics and Paralympics" was unveiled in a star-studded ceremony in London. The logo, designed by Wolff Ollins, depicts a jagged emblem based on the date 2012. The word "London" appears in the first digit of the 2012 date, while the five Olympic rings are included in the second digit. "This is the vision at the very heart of our brand. It will define the venues we build and the Games we hold and act as a reminder of our promise to use the Olympic spirit to inspire everyone and reach out to young people around the world. It is an invitation to take part and be involved. We will host a Games where everyone is invited to join in because they are inspired by the Games to either take part in the many sports, cultural, educational and community events leading up to 2012 or they will be inspired to achieve personal goals," said Lord Coe (Chairman of the 2012 London 2012 organizing committee). "London 2012 will be a great sporting summer but will also allow Britain to showcase itself to the world," added Tony Blair, the British Prime Minister.

Did You Know That?
For the first time the same logo will be used for both the Olympic and Paralympic Games when London hosts the 2012 Olympics.

✳ SPECTATOR BECOMES DOUBLE CHAMPION ✳

In 1896 John Boland, an Oxford undergraduate, travelled to Athens, Greece to attend the first modern Olympic Games as a spectator. However, his friend Thrasyvoalos Manaos, Secretary of the Athens 1896 organizing committee, entered Boland into the tennis competition and he won two events, the men's singles and the men's doubles. In the first round of the singles Boland defeated Friedrich Traun, a German who had been earlier eliminated from the 800 metres. Boland and Traun then teamed up for the doubles event, defeating their Egyptian/Greek opponents in the final after losing the first set.

✳ BRITAIN'S FIRST ROWING MASTER ✳

During the Stockholm Olympics of 1912, Ewart Douglas Horsfall won his first two gold medals for Great Britain in rowing. He was considered Britain's greatest ever rower prior to Steve Redgrave's domination of the sport.

�֎ CARL LEWIS (1961–) ✷

Frederick Carlton "Carl" Lewis was born on 1 July 1961 in Birmingham, Alabama, but grew up in Willingboro, New Jersey. Carl's father William encouraged Carl with his athletics and often told him stories about the legendary Jesse Owens. When Carl finally met Owens, at a track event in the early 1970s, the four times Olympic gold medallist from the 1936 Berlin Olympics told Carl to "have fun". When he was 13 years old Carl began to compete in the long jump, and in 1979 he broke the high school long jump record with a leap of 8.13m (26ft 8in). In Houston he was coached by Tom Tellez, who was to stay at his side during his entire athletics career. In 1980 Lewis qualified for the USA Olympic team in the long jump event and as a member of their 4x100m relay team. Disappointingly, the USA-led boycott of the Games meant that all American athletes stayed at home. In 1981 he became the fastest sprinter in the world when he ran the 100m in 10.00 seconds, but he had not yet tested himself in a major international competition. In 1983 he participated in the inaugural IAAF World Championships held in Helsinki, Finland, and returned home a superstar with three gold medals, having won the long jump, the 100m and the 4x100m relay (in a new world record time). On 14 May 1983 he became the first athlete to break the 10-second barrier for 100m at low altitude, clocking 9.97 seconds.

At the 1984 Los Angeles Olympics Lewis claimed four gold medals: he won the 100m (9.99 seconds), the long jump (8.54m) and the 200m (19.80 seconds, a new Olympic record), and then equalled Jesse Owens's gold medal haul at an Olympiad when he anchored the USA team to gold in the 4x100m (37.83 seconds, a new world record). For the third consecutive year he was voted the Athlete of the Year by *Track and Field News*. At the 1987 World Championships in Rome he retained all three gold medals he won in Helsinki, and at the 1988 Seoul Olympics he retained his 100m title (after Ben Johnson was stripped of the gold) and helped the USA to gold in the 4x100m relay. At the 1992 Olympics in Barcelona Lewis won gold in the long jump and gold in the 4x100m, and four years later in Atlanta, he won his fourth consecutive Olympic long jump gold medal, bringing his career tally to nine Olympic golds and one Olympic silver, plus ten World Championships medals (eight gold, one silver and one bronze).

Did You Know That?
In 1984 Carl Lewis was selected in the 10th round of the NBA draft by the Chicago Bulls (the same year that the Bulls picked Michael Jordan in the first round). Lewis never played a game in the NBA.

✳ OLYMPIC TALK (23) ✳

"When I passed the Chancellor he arose, waved his hand at me, and I waved back at him. I think the writers showed bad taste in criticizing the man of the hour in Germany."
Jesse Owens, winner of four gold medals at the 1936 Olympics

✳ NOTABLE OLYMPIC ACHIEVEMENTS ✳

Most medals
Women: 18: Larysa Latynina (USSR), gymnastics, 1956–64;
Men: 15: Nikolai Andrianov (USSR), gymnastics, 1972–80.

Most gold medals in individual events
Men: 8: Ray Ewry (USA), athletics, 1900–08;
Women: 7: Vera Caslavska (Cze), gymnastics, 1964–68.

Most consecutive victories in an individual event
Men: 4: Paul Elvstrom (Den), Finn class sailing, 1948–60; Al
Oerter (USA), discus, 1956–68; Carl Lewis (USA), long jump, 1984–96.
Women: 3: Larysa Latynina (USSR), floor exercise, 1956–64; Dawn
Fraser (Aus) 100m freestyle, 1956–64; Krisztina Egerszegi (Hun) 200m
backstroke, 1988–96.

Most consecutive victories in same event, team
6: Aladar Gerevich (Hun), team sabre fencing, 1932–60.

Most gold medals
Men: 9: Paavo Nurmi (Fin), athletics 1920–28; Mark Spitz (USA),
swimming, 1968–72; Carl Lewis (USA), athletics, 1984–96;
Women: Larysa Latynina (USSR), gymnastics, 1956–64.

Most medals in individual events
Women: 14 Larysa Latynina (USSR), gymnastics, 1956–64;
Men: 12: Nikolai Andrianov (USSR), gymnastics, 1972–80.

Youngest medal winners in an individual event
Women: 12 years 24 days: Inge Sorensen (Den), 200m breaststroke, 1936;
Men: 14 years 11 days: Nils Skoglund (Den), high diving, 1920.

Youngest gold medal winners
Women: 13 years 268 days: Marjroie Gestring (USA), diving, 1936;
Men: 13 years 283 days: Klaus Zerta (Ger), rowing, 1960.

❋ OLYMPIC TORCH RELAY ❋

For the ancient Greeks fire had divine connotations as it was thought to have been stolen by Prometheus from the Greek god Zeus. The modern torch relay was introduced by Carl Diem, the president of the organizing committee for the Berlin Olympics of 1936. Diem's idea was part of an effort to turn the games into a glorification of the Third Reich. However, despite its origin the torch relay ceremony still exists. Nowadays the Olympic torch is lit several months before the opening ceremony of an Olympiad on the site of the ancient Olympics in Olympia, Greece. The igniting ceremony is performed by 11 women (representing the roles of priestesses), and the Olympic torch is lit by the sun's rays aided by the use of a parabolic mirror. Next the flame is handed over to the officials of the host city in a ceremony held in the Panathinaiko Stadium, Athens, which marks the beginning of the torch relay. The torch is then transported to the host city of the next Olympiad by a variety of means, including air transport as well as on foot in the traditional way. Other unusual means of transportation have included divers, a camel, an electronic pulse and a Native American canoe. The Olympic torch relay ends on the day of the official opening ceremony in the main stadium playing host to the Games. After being ignited, the Olympic flame continues to burn in a specially made cauldron throughout the Games and is extinguished following the closing ceremony.

❋ TWO SILVERS, NO GOLD ❋

At Stockholm 1912 Anders Ahlgren of Sweden fought Finland's Ivar Bohling in the final of the wrestling middleweight B class. The pair wrestled for nine hours without a winner emerging, and the officials declared the match a tie. Neither of the two was awarded a gold medal, both receiving silver medals instead.

❋ "THE GAMES MUST GO ON!" ❋

The Munich Games were suspended for 34 hours after the murder of 11 Israeli athletes by the Black September terrorist organization on 5 September 1972. The day after the massacre a mass was held in Munich's Olympiastadion to commemorate the victims, and the flags of all the competing nations were flown at half-mast. However, while many athletes returned home and others called for the Games to be ended, the 84-year-old outgoing IOC President, Avery Brundage, famously insisted, "The Games must go on!"

✳ THE POPULAR BEAR CUB ✳

"Misha", the official mascot of the 1980 Moscow Olympics, was perhaps the most successful of all the IOC's Olympic mascots. The bear cub was used extensively during the opening and closing ceremonies, was made into a TV animated cartoon and appeared on a large number and variety of merchandise products.

✳ ANYONE FOR TENNIS? ✳

Lawn tennis was an event included in the inaugural modern Olympic Games held in Athens in 1896, but after the 1924 Games held in Paris the sport was dropped. In 1968 and in 1984 tennis returned to the Summer Games as a demonstration sport, and in 1988 it was again given accreditation as a full medal sport.

✳ THE LIDDELL MEMORIAL ✳

In 1991 a small memorial headstone was unveiled by Edinburgh University at Eric Liddell's previously unmarked grave in the Tientsin province of North China. Paying tribute to the athlete who won the 400m gold medal for Great Britain at the 1924 Paris Olympics, a few simple words taken from the Book of Isaiah were engraved on the memorial: "They shall mount up with wings as eagles; they shall run and not be weary."

✳ INTERCALATED GAMES ✳

In 1906 Baron Pierre de Coubertin permitted Greece to stage an Intercalated Games in Athens as compensation for the country losing the right to host every Summer Olympics. Although the International Olympic Committee does not officially recognize the 1906 Games, despite the fact that they were organized by them, many historians consider the 1906 Intercalated Games as a proper Olympics.

Did You Know That?
Great Britain won eight gold, 11 silver and six bronze medals at the 1906 Games in Athens.

✳ A CLASSIC ATHLETE ✳

At the London Olympics of 1948, Micheline Ostermeyer, a French concert pianist, won both the discus throw and the shot put.

❊ THE GAMES OF THE XXVI OLYMPIAD ❊

The Games of the XXVI Olympiad were held in Atlanta, Georgia, USA on what was the 100th anniversary of the modern Olympics. On 19 July 1996, President Bill Clinton officially opened the Games in the purpose-built 85,000-seater Centennial Olympic Stadium, with the Olympic flame lit by perhaps the best-known sportsman in the world, the legendary boxer Muhammad Ali. The Olympic oath was taken by Teresa Edwards (basketball) and the officials' oath by Hobie Billingsly (diving). However, just eight days into the Games a terrorist bomb exploded during a concert in the Centennial Olympic Park, killing one person, causing the death of another from a heart attack and injuring a further 110 people. The Games organizing committee was criticized for the excessive commercialism of the Olympics, which did make a profit, but the Olympiad is best remembered for some remarkable sporting achievements. With his long jump victory Carl Lewis (USA) became only the third person in Olympic history to win the same individual event four times and the fourth person to earn a ninth gold medal. On the track, Michael Johnson (USA) broke the 200m world record (he ran 19.32 seconds) on his way to becoming the first athlete to win both the 200m gold medal and the 400m gold medal at a single Olympiad. In weightlifting, Naim Suleymanoglu from Turkey became the first weightlifter to win three Olympic gold medals. All 179 NOCs sent athletes to the Games, with a total of 10,318 (6,806 men, 3,512 women) participating in 271 events across 26 sports. A record-breaking 79 nations won medals, with 53 claiming at least one gold medal. At the closing ceremony on 4 August 1996, the media quickly picked up on IOC President Juan Antonio Samaranch's speech in which he said, "Well done Atlanta", rather than calling the Olympiad the best yet, which he had done at every previous Games during his presidency.

Atlanta 1996 – Final Medals Table (Top 10)

Pos.	Nation	Gold	Silver	Bronze	Total
1	USA	44	32	25	101
2	Russian Federation	26	21	16	63
3	Germany	20	18	27	65
4	China	16	22	12	50
5	France	15	7	15	37
6	Italy	13	10	12	35
7	Australia	9	9	23	41
8	Cuba	9	8	8	25
9	Ukraine	9	2	12	23
10	South Korea	7	15	5	27

❋ THE OLYMPIC CREED ❋

"The most important thing in the Olympic Games is not to win but to take part, just as the most important thing in life is not the triumph but the struggle. The essential thing is not to have conquered but to have fought well." These words were first uttered by Bishop Ethelbert Talbote, Bishop of Central Pennsylvania, in a guest sermon in St Paul's Cathedral. When Pierre de Coubertin heard the Bishop's words he made them the Olympic motto.

❋ THE FIRST OLYMPIC FIRE ❋

Fire did not appear at the modern Olympics until the Amsterdam Games of 1928. Jan Wils, the man who designed the Olympic Stadium in Amsterdam, included a tower (the Marathon Tower) in his design for the stadium and had the idea that a flame would burn throughout the duration of the Games. On 28 July 1928, an employee of the Amsterdam electricity board lit the first Olympic fire in the Marathon Tower.

Did You Know That?
The Marathon Tower was nicknamed "KLM's ashtray" by the people of Amsterdam (KLM is the Royal Dutch airline).

❋ MARY LOU'S GOLD ❋

At the 1984 Games Mary Lou Retton of the USA became the first gymnast from outside Eastern Europe to win the women's gymnastics all-around competition. However, because of the Soviet-led boycott of the Games, only one of the 11 women who won a gold medal at the 1983 World Gymnastics Championships in Budapest competed in Los Angeles (Romania's Ecaterina Szabo). In Budapest Szabo won the gold medal in the floor exercise, but in Los Angeles she won gold medals in the balance beam (tied), the floor exercise and the vault, as well as the team gold, plus a silver medal in the all-around.

❋ FROM RIGHT TO LEFT TO GOLD ❋

In 1938 Karoly Takacs was a member of Hungary's world champion pistol shooting team when a grenade shattered his right hand. Takacs, a right-handed pistol shooter, then taught himself to shoot with his left hand, and at London in 1948 he won the gold medal in the rapid-fire pistol event.

✳ OLYMPIC TALK (24) ✳

"I hope I will be partly excused by the fact that I was simply an Indian schoolboy and did not know all about such things. In fact, I did not know that I was doing wrong, because I was doing what I knew several other college men had done, except that they did not use their own names."

Extract from **Jim Thorpe's** *letter to the AAU in 1913 explaining his "professional" status as a baseball player*

✳ NO GOLD FOR THE HOSTS ✳

At the Montreal Games of 1976, the host nation Canada managed to win only five silver and six bronze medals. This was the first and, to date, the only time in Olympic history that the hosts failed to claim a single gold medal at the Games.

✳ OLYMPIC EVENTS OR CHAMPIONSHIPS? ✳

The term "Olympic Games" was replaced by "Concours Internationaux d'exercises physiques et de sport" in the official report of the sporting events of the 1900 World's Fair, which was held in conjunction with the Paris Olympics of 1900. Meanwhile at the same Games of the II Olympiad, many of the press in attendance reported competitions variously as "International Championships", "International Games", "Paris Championships", "World Championships" and "Grand Prix of the Paris Exposition". Baron de Coubertin is reported to have said, in an interview after the Paris Games: "It's a miracle that the Olympic Movement survived that celebration."

✳ THE 1900 GAMES MEDAL ✳

The front of the 1900 medal shows a winged goddess with her arms raised and holding laurel branches in both hands, while behind her is a view of Paris and the monuments of the Exposition Universelle. On the back a victorious athlete is depicted standing on a podium with his arm raised, holding a laurel branch in his right hand. A stadium and the Acropolis of Athens can be seen in the background.

✳ CHINA WIN ANTHEM GOLD ✳

The Republic of China's "Three Principles of the People" was chosen as the best national anthem at the 1936 Games.

❈ BIRTH OF THE OLYMPIC MOVEMENT ❈

When Pierre de Coubertin announced in Paris in 1892 that he intended to re-establish the Olympic Games, he was applauded by all in attendance, but few actually realized the enormity of the tasks that lay ahead in organizing an Olympiad. The International Olympic Committee (IOC) was created on 23 June 1894; the first Olympic Games of the modern era opened in Athens on 6 April 1896; and the Olympic Movement has gone from strength to strength ever since. The Olympic Movement includes the IOC, Organizing Committees of the Olympic Games (OCOGs), the National Olympic Committees (NOCs), the International Federations (IFs), the national associations, clubs and, last but certainly not least, the athletes. It is the responsibility of the Olympic Movement to pull together all those who agree to be guided by the Olympic Charter and who recognize the authority of the IOC. The overall goal of the Olympic Movement is to contribute to building a peaceful and better world by educating youth through sport practised without discrimination of any kind, in a spirit of friendship, solidarity and fair play.

❈ FOOTBALL FIRST ❈

In 1900 football became the first team event to be introduced to the modern Games. Great Britain, represented in Paris by Upton Park FC, beat the host nation France 4–0 in the final.

❈ NO WOMEN ALLOWED ❈

Women were not allowed to compete in the 1896 Games at Athens, but one woman, a protester named Stamata Revithi, ran the marathon route the day after Greece's Spyridon Louis won the event.

❈ JAPAN'S GYMNASTICS MASTER ❈

In Montreal Sawao Kato from Japan won the gold medal in the parallel bars and in the team event, plus a silver medal in the all-around competition. These three medals brought his Olympic medal tally to 12: eight gold, three silver and one bronze. This not only made him the most successful male gymnast at the Olympics, and the most successful Japanese Olympian, but he also joined an elite club, becoming one of only ten athletes to have won eight or more Olympic gold medals.

❋ THE OLYMPIC FLAG ❋

In 1913 Baron Pierre de Coubertin designed a flag for the 1914 Congress of the Olympic Movement in Paris, and in particular to celebrate its 20th anniversary. De Coubertin, the French founder of the modern Games, is said to have discovered the original Olympic symbol of five rings engraved on an altar-stone unearthed at Delphi, but some writers on the Games refute this claim. Robert Knight Barney (in an article entitled "This Great Symbol: the Tricks of History" published in *Olympic Review* in 1992), indicates that de Coubertin probably got the idea from the French sports federation USFSA (Union des Sociétés Françaises des Sports Athlétiques), which used an emblem consisting of two interlocking rings. For his 1913 creation de Coubertin chose five interlocking rings, and it has been claimed that he did this to celebrate the first five modern Games of the Olympiads I, II, III, IV and V. As colours for the five rings he chose those of the flags of all the countries that were part of the International Olympic Movement at the time. In total he used six colours: white for the cloth representing "no borders" and black, blue, green, red and yellow for the rings. The 1914 Congress was so in awe of the flag that the design was unanimously adopted as the flag for the International Olympic Movement. The five rings symbolize the five Olympic continents, although no continent is represented by any specific ring, and are intertwined on the flag, forming a trapezium with the blue, black and red rings on top and the yellow and green rings at the bottom.

Did You Know That?
Whereas white was chosen to represent no borders across the five continents, the flag used at the Antwerp Olympics in 1920 and the flag used in the Seoul Olympics in 1988 both had a fringe of the six colours around the white field.

❋ FAMOUS FOR BEING LAST ❋

During the 1968 Games John Stephen Akhwari came last in the marathon but achieved stardom in his native Tanzania for having finished the race despite suffering a dislocated knee in the course of it.

❋ MEXICO'S TRIPLE TREBLE ❋

At the Mexico City Games the host nation won three gold medals, three silver medals and three bronze medals.

❋ THE LATIN GAMES ❋

Mexico City 1968 is the only Olympiad ever held in Latin America and was only the second ever Olympics not to be held either in Europe, Australia or the USA.

❋ ABRAHAMS AND LIDDELL ❋

While Abrahams won the 100m gold medal, his team-mate Eric Liddell won gold in the 400 metres in a new world record time of 47.6 seconds. Both athletes also participated in the 200 metres, with Liddell taking the bronze medal and Abrahams coming in sixth and last. Fifty-six years later, Scotland's Allan Wells won the 100m gold medal in the Moscow Olympics. Following his victory Wells was asked if he had run the race for Harold Abrahams, the last British Olympic champion at 100 metres, to which Wells quietly replied, "No, this one was for Eric Liddell." Liddell was born in Tientsin, North China, the second son of Revd and Mrs James Dunlop Liddell, who were Scottish missionaries.

❋ THE WHITE CITY ❋

Work on the White City Stadium, situated in Shepherd's Bush in West London, began in 1906 as soon as London was awarded the Olympic Games of 1908 after the original hosts Rome withdrew. Built specifically to host the Games of the IV Olympiad, amazingly the first all-purpose stadium was constructed in a relatively short period of time. At the time it was widely regarded as a technological marvel. It held 68,000 people and contained a running track that was 24 foot wide and enclosed by a 35 foot wide, 660 yard long cycle track. In 1985 the stadium was demolished to make way for a new building, BBC White City.

❋ THE HEAD WAITER ❋

In the final of the 800 metres in Munich, Dave Wottle of the USA won the gold medal in one of the most unusual races ever run by an athlete. Wottle was at the back of the field for the first 600 metres of the race and then started to move up the gears, gradually overtaking one runner after another. He took the lead in the final metres of the race and hung on to it to win his gold medal by a slender 0.03 seconds from the favourite, the USSR's Yevgeny Arzhonov. His smooth progress to victory earned him the nickname "the Head Waiter".

✳ THE GAMES OF THE XXVII OLYMPIAD ✳

The Games of the XXVII Olympiad were held in Sydney, Australia, in 2000 and were the biggest Games to date. The opening ceremony took place on 15 September 2000 with the Games officially opened by Sir William Deane, Governor-General of Australia, at Stadium Australia. Cathy Freeman (athletics) lit the Olympic flame, the Olympic oath was performed by hockey player Rechelle Hawkes, and the officials' oath was taken by Peter Kerr (water polo). Every IOC member nation participated in the Olympiad except for Afghanistan, which had been suspended by the IOC because of the ruling Taliban's prohibition of all sports participation. Korea (South Korea) and the Democratic People's Republic of Korea (North Korea) marched together under the same flag although the athletes competed separately. The Games witnessed a number of firsts and some outstanding individual athletic performances. For the first time tests to detect EPO and blood tests were conducted; taekwondo and the triathlon were added to the Olympic programme; Colombia claimed its first ever gold medal; Vietnam won its first Olympic medal; Susanthika Jayasinghe became the first Sri Lankan female to win a medal, and women took part in the modern pentathlon and weightlifting for the first time in Olympic history. Individually, Birgit Fischer became the first woman in any sport (kayak) to win Olympic medals 20 years apart, while Steve Redgrave became the first rower to win gold medals at five consecutive Olympiads. In total 199 nations (excluding East Timor, whose four athletes competed under the IOA banner) sent 10,651 athletes (6,582 men, 4,069 women) to compete in 300 events across 28 sports. In his closing address the outgoing IOC President, Juan Antonio Samaranch, said: "I am proud and happy to proclaim that you have presented to the world the best Olympic Games ever."

Sydney 2000 – Final Medals Table (Top 10)

Pos.	Nation	Gold	Silver	Bronze	Total
1	USA	40	24	33	97
2	Russia	32	28	28	88
3	China	28	16	15	59
4	Australia	16	25	17	58
5	Germany	13	17	26	56
6	France	13	14	11	38
7	Italy	13	8	13	34
8	Netherlands	12	9	4	25
9	Cuba	11	11	7	29
10	Great Britain	11	10	7	28

※ WEIGHTLIFTING HERO ※

Turkey's Naim Suleymanoglu became the first weightlifter in the sport's history to win three consecutive Olympic gold medals when he took the 59–64kg division at Atlanta. Suleymanoglu is hugely popular in Turkey, as a journalist at the Games confirmed: "When he eats at a restaurant, nobody asks him to pay the bill; if he breaks the speed limit, he does not get fined, and the police wish him a pleasant journey."

※ ATHLETES WIN COINS ※

Up until 1991, Australia minted one-cent and two-cent bronze coins, but these coins were removed from general circulation in 1992. The coins were then melted down and turned into bronze medals, which were presented at the 2000 Olympics.

※ KEEPING THINGS IN SYNCH ※

Thomas Bimis and Nikolaos Siranidis won Greece's first ever Olympic medal in diving by taking the gold medal in the synchronized springboard event at the Athens Olympics.

※ TO COMPETE OR NOT TO COMPETE ※

In the opening ceremony of the 1980 Games, 15 national teams – Andorra, Australia, Belgium, Denmark, France, Great Britain, Ireland, Italy, Luxembourg, Netherlands, Portugal, Puerto Rico, San Marino, Spain and Switzerland – marched under the Olympic flag as opposed to their national flags. As their athletes officially competed under the Olympic flag, the Olympic hymn was used at the appropriate medal ceremonies. New Zealand, however, competed under the New Zealand Olympic and Commonwealth Games Association flag. In protest against the USSR's invasion of Afghanistan in December 1979, there was a USA-led 64-country boycott of the Games. These 15 countries, however, left it to their athletes to decide whether to compete.

※ NADIA TRUMPED BY KORNELIA ※

Although 14-year-old Nadia Comaneci (Romania) was the undoubted darling of the 1976 Games in Montreal, scoring seven perfect 10.00s en route to winning three gold medals in gymnastics, East Germany's Kornelia Ender won four gold medals in the pool.

12345678

Lane No./Athlete	Country	Olympic Medals
1 Gabrielle Dorio	Italy	Gold – Los Angeles 1984, Silver – Moscow 1980
2 Kelly Holmes	Great Britain	Gold – Athens 2004
3 Hassiba Boulmerka	Algeria	Gold – Barcelona 1992
4 Paula Ivan	Romania	Gold – Seoul 1988
5 Lyudmila Bragina	Soviet Union	Gold – Munich 1972
6 Svetlana Masterkova	Russia	Gold – Atlanta 1996
7 Nouria Merah-Benida	Algeria	Gold – Sydney 2000
8 Tatyana Kazankina	Soviet Union	Gold – Montreal 1976, Moscow 1980

❀ OLYMPIC TALK (25) ❀

"I have always believed that Harold Abrahams was the only European sprinter who could have run with Jesse Owens, Ralph Metcalfe and the other great sprinters from the US. He was in their class, not only because of natural gifts – his magnificent physique, his splendid racing temperament, his flair for the big occasion; but because he understood athletics, and had given more brainpower and more willpower to the subject than any other runner of his day."

Philip Noel-Baker, Britain's 1912 Olympic captain and a Nobel Prize winner, reflecting in 1948 on Abrahams's athleticism

❀ ORDERS TO SHOOT ❀

On 11 September 1972, a small plane was stolen at Stuttgart airport and the German authorities received information that it was another terrorist attack following on from the massacre in Munich that occurred less than one week earlier. It was claimed that Arab terrorists were planning to drop a bomb on the closing ceremony of the Games, taking place the same day. Georg Leber, the German defence minister, ordered two fighter jets to shadow the aircraft and shoot it down if it approached Munich. During the mayhem radar contact with the plane was lost briefly before another aircraft showed up on the radar system. However, this plane turned out to be a civilian passenger plane, and the stolen plane simply disappeared and was never found.

❀ FIRST STAY-AWAY ATHLETES ❀

Long before the boycotted Games in Moscow (1980) and Los Angeles (1984), tension across Europe at the time stemming from the Russo-Japanese War meant that many of the world's top international athletes did not travel across the Atlantic for the 1904 Olympics in St Louis.

❀ A FIT FAMILY ❀

At Tokyo in 1964 Great Britain's Ann Packer won a silver medal in the 400 metres and a gold medal in the 800 metres. Her fiancé, Robbie Brightwell, also competed in Tokyo and won a silver medal as part of Great Britain's 4x400m relay team. The pair later married and had three sons, two of whom, David and Ian, played professional football for Manchester City.

❋ SIR STEPHEN REDGRAVE, CBE (1962–) ❋

Stephen "Steve" Geoffrey Redgrave was born on 23 March 1962 in Marlow, England, and is widely considered to be Great Britain's greatest ever Olympian, winning five gold medals and a bronze in five successive Olympiads. Only four other Olympians have won gold medals at five or more Olympiads: Aladar Gerevich (six successive Games), Pal Kovacs (five), Reiner Klinke (five) and Brigit Fischer (five). In 1984, at the Los Angeles Olympics, Steve claimed the first of his gold medals for the coxed fours with Martin Cross, Adrian Ellison, Andy Holmes and Richard Budgett. Four years later in Seoul came gold medal number two with partner Andy Holmes in the coxless pairs, plus a bronze medal in the coxed pairs with Holmes and Patrick Sweeney. At the 1992 Barcelona Olympics Steve won his third successive Olympic gold when he rowed to victory in the coxless pairs with Matthew Pinsent. The partnership flourished again at the next Olympiad, Atlanta 1996, retaining their gold in the event. After winning that fourth successive gold in the Atlanta Games, Steve was asked if he would compete in the 2000 Olympics in Sydney. The 34-year-old Redgrave then came out with his famous line, broadcast live on BBC television: "Anyone who sees me go anywhere near a boat again, ever, you've got my permission to shoot me." In 1997 Steve reversed his decision and announced that he would be seeking a fifth successive gold in Sydney. At the 2000 Sydney Games he won gold medal number five in the coxless four with James Cracknell, Tim Foster and Pinsent. It was rarely easy: in four of his successful finals the winning margin was two seconds or less.

Redgrave had an intensity about rowing that had never been seen before and may never be seen again. He was determined to win every race he entered, and usually was found on the top step of the medal podium, regardless of the status of the tournament. Steve also won nine gold medals, two silver and one bronze in the World Championships and a silver medal in the Junior World Championships. He was named BBC Sports Personality of the Year in 2000 and was awarded the Thomas Keller Medal for Outstanding International Rowing Career by FISA in 2001. He was made an MBE in 1987, awarded the CBE in 1997 and knighted in 2001. His combined haul of 14 Olympic and World Championship gold medals is unsurpassed by any other rower in the sport's long history.

Did You Know That?

In April 2006, Steve Redgrave completed his third London Marathon and raised a record £1.8 million for charity.

❋ GOLDEN GLOVES ❋

The greatest ever Olympic boxing team to represent the USA at an Olympiad is without question the team they sent to the 1976 Montreal Olympics. Five of the team returned home with gold medals: Leo Randolph won the flyweight gold, Howard Davis Jr the lightweight gold, Sugar Ray Leonard the light-welterweight gold, Michael Spinks the middleweight gold and Leon Spinks the light-heavyweight gold. All except Davis went on to become professional World Champions.

❋ A RECORD OLYMPICS ❋

During the Moscow Games, 36 world records, 39 European records and 74 Olympic records were set. Meanwhile, more than five million people attended the various events at the Games, 1.5 million more than the 1976 Olympiad in Montreal.

❋ FIVE DISQUALIFIED ❋

At the 1996 Olympics five athletes were disqualified after tests showed they were taking banned substances. However, several athletes who had originally been banned were reinstated because the drug they were taking had been declared illegal by the IOC only one week before the Olympics commenced.

❋ LADIES DO IT IN UNDER FOUR MINUTES ❋

In the 4x100m swimming medley relay the USA team became the first women's relay team to swim under four minutes, claiming the gold medal in a new world record time of 3:58.30. The swimming quad comprised B. J. Bedford, Megan Quann (Jendrick), Jenny Thompson and Dara Torres.

❋ TAYLAN PROVIDES DELIGHT FOR TURKEY ❋

In the ladies' weightlifting competition at the 2004 Athens Olympics, Turkey's Nurcan Taylan won the gold medal in the 48kg category. Amazingly, Taylan lifted a new world record of 97.5kg in the snatch, double her bodyweight, and 112.5kg in the clean and jerk on her way to the gold medal and a new world record with a combined score of 210kg. She became the first Turkish woman in any sport to win an Olympic gold.

⁂ THE GAMES OF THE XXVIII OLYMPIAD ⁂

In 2004 the Games of the XXVIII Olympiad returned to Athens, in Greece, the home of the ancient Games and the setting for the first modern Games in 1896. Athens beat competition from rival IOC bidders Buenos Aires, Cape Town, Rome and Stockholm to win the right to host the Games. The Athens Olympics were officially opened in the city's Olympic Stadium on 13 August 2004 by the President of the Hellenic Republic, Konstantinos Stephanopoulos. The Olympic flame was lit by six torchbearers: Nikos Galis (basketball), Dimitrios Domazos (football), Paraskevi Patoulidou (athletics), Akakios Kachiasvilis (weightlifting), Ioannis Melissanidis (artistic gymnastics) and Nikolaos Kaklamanakis (sailing). The Olympic oath was performed by 19-year-old Zoi Dimoschaki (swimming) and the officials' oath was taken by Lazaros Voreadis (basketball). A total of 11,099 athletes from 201 different countries, a record attendance, participated in 301 medal events across 28 different sports – one more than in Sydney 2000 – while an estimated worldwide audience of 3.9 billion people followed every move on television in the comfort of their homes. A number of notable firsts happened at the Games: Kiribati and Timor Leste entered teams for the first time; double trap shooter Ahmed Almaktoum won the first gold medal for the United Arab Emirates; Ilias Iliadis claimed Greece's first ever gold medal in judo; Thai weightlifter Pawina Thongsuk became the first woman from her country to win a gold medal, and women's wrestling was included in the programme for the first time. The outstanding athlete of the Games was the American swimmer Michael Phelps, who won six gold medals and established a new single-Games record by collecting eight medals in total. The closing ceremony took place on 29 August 2004.

Athens 2004 – Final Medals Table (Top 10)

Pos.	*Nation*	*Gold*	*Silver*	*Bronze*	*Total*
1	USA	36	39	27	102
2	China	32	17	14	63
3	Russia	27	27	38	92
4	Australia	17	16	16	49
5	Japan	16	9	12	37
6	Germany	13	16	20	49
7	France	11	9	13	33
8	Italy	10	11	11	32
9	South Korea	9	12	9	30
10	Great Britain	9	9	12	30

❊ LOSERS TURN WINNERS ❊

In 1970 Montreal was awarded the right to host the Olympic Games of 1976. The Canadians defeated the rival bids of Moscow and Los Angeles although those cities hosted the next two Games, Moscow in 1980 and Los Angeles in 1984.

❊ MERCENARY BOXER ❊

At the 1956 Games, Laszlo Papp from Hungary became the first boxer to win three successive gold medals at an Olympiad. The following year he turned professional but could not fight in his own country as Hungary was a communist state and professional boxing was not permitted. Papp was forced to travel to Vienna to train and had to stage all of his fights outside Hungary. He won the European middleweight title and, in 1964, earned the chance to fight for the world middleweight title. Sadly, Papp was denied an exit visa because the Hungarian government resented the fact that he had managed to fight professionally by staging his fights outside the country. Papp was undefeated in the ring, with 27 wins and two draws (15 of his wins by way of knockout). In 2001 he was inducted into the International Boxing Hall of Fame.

❊ IOC BANS USA DELEGATE ❊

Prior to the start of the 1936 Berlin Olympics, the IOC expelled committee member Ernest Lee Jahnke of the USA, the son of a German immigrant, who openly encouraged athletes to boycott the games. Jahnke's position in the IOC was taken by the USA's NOC president, Avery Brundage.

❊ TENNIS PROS ❊

As a direct result of the difficulties determining the amateur status of players, tennis was taken off the list of Olympic events after the 1924 Games in Paris and was not included again until Seoul 1988.

❊ SUMMER NOT WINTER ❊

The proposal for a winter sports week for the Stockholm Olympics featuring figure skating was rejected by the Swedish organizers because they preferred to promote the Nordic Games, a quadrennial sporting event, instead.

❊ OLYMPIC TALK (26) ❊

"The most important thing in the Olympic Games is not winning but taking part; the essential thing in life is not conquering but fighting well."

Pierre de Coubertin, *the founder of the modern Olympics, at the 1908 Olympic Games held in London*

❊ MIND THE DUCKS, PLEASE ❊

At Amsterdam in 1928 Australia's Bobby Pearce encountered an unusual hazard midway through his single sculls quarter-final race against France's Victor Saurin. To the young Sydney rower's astonishment a family of ducks lay in front of him in the water. Pearce allowed the ducks to pass in front of his boat in single file before continuing to row, and proceeded to win the race to enthusiastic applause from spectators for his actions. In the final, Pearce beat Kenneth Myers of the USA by the huge margin of 9.8 seconds. After the Games Pearce hoped that his Olympic gold medal victory would gain him admission to row in the Diamond Sculls at Henley. However, the organizers refused the young Australian permission to race because his occupation was not a professional one: he was a carpenter and therefore deemed to be a labourer. Things went from bad to worse for Pearce when he was unable to secure work in Sydney as a result of the economic depression prevalent in the country at the time. However, Lord Dewar, the Canadian whisky manufacturer, learned of Pearce's bad luck and gave him a job as a salesman, an occupation that made him eligible for Henley. In 1931 he travelled to London and won the Diamond Sculls by six lengths, and at the Los Angeles Games of 1932 he retained his Olympic championship, thus becoming the first rower to win two singles sculls gold medals.

❊ *JEU DE PAUME* ❊

Jeu de paume, or real tennis as it is better known, was an event contested for the first and only time as a medal event at the 1908 Olympics. The competition was held in the Queen's Club in West Kensington and was won by Jay Gould II (USA) with Great Britain's Eustace Miles and Neville Lytton winning the silver and bronze medals respectively. An outdoor version of the game called *Longue paume* was a demonstration sport at the 1900 Olympics and later an exhibition event at the 1924 Olympics.

❋ THE ANCIENT OLYMPIC GAMES ❋

The original Olympic Games began in 776 BC and were held in Olympia, Greece. The Games were abolished in AD 393 and were not held again until a French nobleman, Baron Pierre de Coubertin, revived them in 1896.

❋ AN ARTISTIC SWIMMER ❋

Alfred Hajos from Hungary, a double swimming gold medallist at the first modern Games at Athens in 1896, won the top medal in the architectural division of the 1924 Olympic art contest in Paris. Specializing in sports facilities, Hajos's architecture partner was Dezso Lauber, who played tennis for Hungary in the 1908 Games.

❋ FIRST BLACK GOLD MEDAL WINNER ❋

The Franco-Haitian rugby player Constantin Henriquez de Zubiera became the first black gold medallist when the French representative side won the rugby tournament at the 1900 Paris Olympics. He also competed in the tug of war event at the Games, winning a silver medal for France.

❋ DISGRACED SUPPORT ❋

Two Bulgarian weightlifters were stripped of their gold medals at the 1988 Olympics after failing drugs tests. The Bulgarian team immediately withdrew its athletes from the Olympiad in support of the two disgraced weightlifters.

❋ CAPTAINS FANTASTIC ❋

Linford Christie (GB men's team captain) and Sally Gunnell (GB ladies' team captain) both won gold medals at the 1992 Games in Barcelona. Christie won gold in the 100 metres, and Gunnell in the 400 metres hurdles.

❋ CHINA FINALLY ❋

China finally won the men's Olympic team all-around gymnastics title at the 2000 Games after finishing in the silver medal position for the past two Olympiads. Ukraine claimed the silver medal and Russia the bronze.

✤ BIBLIOGRAPHY AND REFERENCES ✤

WEBSITES

english.people.com ❖ espn.go.com
history1900s.about.com ❖ home.nycap.rr.com
quotations.about.com ❖ virtual.finland.fi
wikipedia.org ❖ www.aafla.org ❖ www.allstates-flag.com
www.britannica.com ❖ www.databaseolympics.com
www.factmonster.com ❖ www.fhw.gr/olympics/ancient
www.fundaciobarcelonaolimpica.es ❖ www.ighof.com
www.jesseowens.com ❖ www.jewishsports.net
www.johnnyweissmuller.ro ❖ www.nostos.com
www.olympic.org ❖ www.sok.se
www.steveredgrave.com ❖ www.times-olympic.co.uk

BOOKS

❖ *The Guinness Book of Olympic Facs and Feats*, Stan Greenberg, 1996, Guinness Publishing, Enfield.

❖ *The Olympics: A History of the Modern Games,* A Guttmann, 1992, University of Illinois Press, Chicago.

❖ *This Great Symbol: Pierre de Coubertin and Origins of the Modern Olympic Games,* John J. MacAloon, 1982, University of Chicago Press, Chicago.

❖ *Eric Liddell: Pure Gold: a New Biography of the Olympic Champion who Inspired Chariot of Fire,* David McCasland, 2003, Discovery House Publishers.

❖ *The Complete Book of the Summer Olympics*, David Wallechinsky, 2000, Overlook Press, Woodstock.

❊ INDEX ❊